# 100% Me

# Amy Childs

## 100% Me

BLINK
bringing you closer

Published by Blink Publishing
107-109 The Plaza,
535 Kings Road,
Chelsea Harbour,
London, SW10 0SZ

www.blinkpublishing.co.uk

facebook.com/blinkpublishing
Twitter.com/blinkpublishing

978-1-910536-47-6

Design by Blink Publishing
Printed and bound by Clays Ltd, St Ives Plc

1 3 5 7 9 10 8 6 4 2

Papers used by Blink Publishing are natural, recyclable products made
from wood grown in sustainable forests. The manufacturing processes
conform to the environmental regulations of the country of origin.

Every reasonable effort has been made to trace copyright holders of
material reproduced in this book, but if any have been inadvertently
overlooked the publishers would be glad to hear from them.

Blink Publishing is an imprint of the Bonnier Publishing Group
www.bonnierpublishing.co.uk

*Dedication*

*For my Nanny Joan*
*who became an angel on 21ˢᵗ April 2012.*

*"If Tears Could Build a Stairway and Memories*
*a Lane I'd Walk Right Up to Heaven*
*and Bring You Back Again."*

*You're an amazing woman and you'll never be*
*forgotten. I miss you every day. I love you.*

# ACKNOWLEDGEMENTS

I've got so many people to thank. Where do I start? Never in a million years did I ever think I could have achieved what I have in such a short space of time. Or ever, TBH*. How the hell have I managed to go from working in a beauticians to owning my own salon, a clothing line and now Amy's Academy? I still can't believe it myself and I'm not sure I ever will because I'm still me and I don't feel any different. I don't feel like a celebrity. I've got a load of gorgies* to thank but the most important thank-you goes to my mum and dad. 100%. Without them none of this would have been possible. I owe everything to them because they sacrificed so much to make sure that I had the best start in life. I hope that when I have kids I can do the same for them and show them the love and belief that Mum and Dad have in me. Even when I was doing proper* bad at school they never had a go at me, they never pressured me or gave me any agg* – they just wanted me to be happy and to do my best. That, they said: 'was all they could ask for.' They really are the best. Mum and Dad – I LOVE you. 🐻

A shout-out to Billy, my brother. He's the best brother and he'll always help me when I'm in trouble. He could have been well jel* of me in *TOWIE*, but he's not like that and he's always been a big support. I love him and I can't wait to meet my little niece or nephew.

I want to also say thanks to my Auntie Karen, Harry's mum. She's like a second mum and she's always been there for me. She'll never take sides, but she's a great listener and I love her to bits. I've grown up with Auntie Karen and her kids are like brothers to me. Harry you all know from *TOWIE* – so you know how close we are. He's my best mate, he's gorge*.

There's been a lot of belief in me over the years and when I met Claire Powell from CAN Management she, too, saw something in me that she wanted to invest in and believe in. I am so grateful for that. Claire has opened more doors for me than I ever thought possible – she knows her stuff and she decided that I was someone she wanted to manage. She put her own money in and gambled it on me. I'm glad it's paid off and that I have hopefully made her proud. To be given the chances I've had is a proper dream.

I can remember going to London with Mum not long after Claire first took me on. She was having a big birthday party and we walked in and we were both like; 'Oh My god!'. We looked across the room and there was Peter Andre standing right there. Me and Mum couldn't believe it. I'd grown up watching him on TV, thinking he was a right sort*. We started to laugh – I think we thought we were in some kind of dream because also standing right there was Gino D'Acampo and Amanda Holden. Literally, it was like we were in a dream and that we were going to wake up at any moment. Unfortunately it wasn't a dream because that night I was papped* outside and I fell over. I was so embarrassed and I hadn't even had a drink! LOL*. Still, it was like a proper dream that at any moment I was going to wake up from but it's never happened and I'm still living that dream – as cheesy as that sounds, it's true. Without the people that work with me and, of course, my amazing fans none of this could or would have been as big as it's become. You are all amazing gorgies and I want to thank you ALL.

Finally, thank you to Hannah Fernando who has helped me to write this book. Words never did come easily to me, honey, and you have done me proud. We had a laugh along the way, didn't we? Our mutual love for Twiglets got us through hours of boring business talk!! I loved our girly time together and our treatments at the salon – it's been major*. 😵‍💫

Finally, finally – thanks to my publisher Blink who have also shown faith in me. It's been brilliant being able to write a book that, I hope, will inspire other people like me to believe in themselves – you don't need to be an A-student boff, you know. Hard work goes a long way.

Go on, give those dreams a go. You CAN do it.

# CONTENTS

INTRODUCTION

# ARE YOU SERIOUS, BABE? I'M FAMOUS…

Where do I begin? It's hard because I still can't believe this has all happened to me… Amy; Amy Childs from Essex. This sort of thing doesn't happen to people like me, it just doesn't.

The idea that I'm here writing my own book for people to read is mad. Totally mad. I don't think I'll ever come to terms with the idea that I'm famous. It even sounds weird using that word. FAMOUS! I swear it's a joke, and one day I'll wake up and this will all have been a dream. An amazing dream but a dream. That's what I keep thinking and I pinch myself, like, at least three times a day. I'm well jel of my own life and I don't think that will ever wear off.

I'm still me, I'm still the girl I always was, I just have a few more quid in my purse and I can't go into town without people stopping me for a selfie or an autograph. Personally, I don't get the fascination – but, love me or hate me, my life has never been better and I'm truly grateful for my incredible life. I will never stop saying 'thank you' to the people around me who had the faith that I could make something of myself, particularly my parents, who have made me who I am.

I'm not gonna lie, every day has it's own challenge and I don't find any of it very easy. This whole thing doesn't come naturally to me. Sitting in business meetings listening to a load of words that aren't 'vajazzle'* or spray-tan related isn't in my comfort zone but each time I'm in one of those types of meetings (I used to try and avoid them as much as possible, I'm better now!) I try to learn something new. My mum once said to me: 'Go on, Ames, just try and take in *one* thing, try and learn *one* thing in every meeting you are in and it'll get easier.' And she was right, it has got a bit easier. This is my life now and I need to try. A few years ago I might have preferred to be somewhere else having my nails done but this is what I do now and, regardless of the challenges, I'm enjoying it and I'm educating myself as I go. I have to because I have a career and staff and salaries to pay. It's bloody scary and a lot of pressure when I think about it. The word 'business' is a boring word isn't it? Well, not anymore – for me anyway. I'd like to think that I bring the fun factor to business and liven up what is a very dull word. Welcome to business the Amy Childs way!

Being serious… as I write this I'm thinking about how my life has changed in such a short space of time. Yes, I'm Amy Childs off of *TOWIE*, but I'm also a successful woman in business and if I can sit through one of those meetings, then so can you. School was so hard for me, I wasn't an A-student, like half of these top businesswomen, or fiercely ambitious –

I was me, the thick-but-glam one who ended up doing good. I hope that I can inspire people like me who never thought they'd get very far in life to have belief in themselves. Luck does play a part, that's true, but the belief that no matter who you are, you can make something of yourself is what will make you stand out from the crowd. Just look at how far I've come... and I want to go even further.

CHAPTER 1

# HOW WELL DO YOU REALLY KNOW ME?

I wanted to start this book by telling you a bit about me. Since I've been on *The Only Way Is Essex* (*TOWIE*) everybody thinks they know me. Did you know that I once had elocution lessons so I spoke all posh? Thought not…

In my head I think people have a certain opinion, based on that one series that I was on the show, and although I loved every part of being on *TOWIE* there's a lot more to Amy Childs! I'm not just all about curlers and fake tan, although that is quite a big part of my life, obvs*!

I'm a lot more ordinary than people probably think and it's the small things in life that make me happy. I can't bear any agg, I like a peaceful life and most of all I like a quiet night in with a glass of prosecco and a good movie.

Beauty has always been my thing… beauty is what I love and is my passion, even from a young age that was obvious, I think. Nothing engaged me in the same way as beauty, like make-up and painting people's nails. It was like it was in me from when I popped into the world on 7<sup>th</sup> June 1990. Don't be shocked, I know everyone thinks I'm older than I am – I'll come back to that later!

I was born in Chadwell Heath in Essex and, as everyone now knows (thanks to *TOWIE*!), Essex can be quite in-your-face when it comes to fashion and looking a certain way all of the time so maybe that was why I loved beauty so much, who knows, but it was that passion that has undoubtedly helped me to get to where I am today. I lived in Chadwell Heath until I was about seven years old. It was just a normal house, nothing fancy because Mum and Dad didn't have much money. I remember everything. It was, like, a little semi-detached house and it wasn't in the best area. It had three bedrooms and mine was painted pink for a princess! What else would you expect? It wasn't in-your-face style-wise – nothing like how we'd do up a house now. It was more understated and there were little jobs that needed doing, like redecorating the bathroom, but my dad, Billy, didn't have a lot of time or money to spend on the house and it didn't bother Billy or me. My brother is also called Billy, BTW* – sorry, that's a bit confusing, isn't it? Things like that don't matter when you're a little kid.

I had a thing about *Barney* – you know, that purple dinosaur that talks? – and the *Teletubbies*, I loved *Teletubbies* but *Barney* I LOVED. When I was four years old I had my tonsils out and I was in so much pain, I can remember it like it was yesterday and Mum (who is called Julie) felt really sorry for me. I wanted a Barney toy but they were out of stock everywhere and Mum hadn't been able to get me one, but that day, after the op, she had obviously searched everywhere and found me my very own Barney and I loved him. I've still bloody got him! It's funny what you remember, but those small things make a kid's childhood, don't they?

Both Mum and Dad worked full-time and worked all the hours so that me and Billy didn't go without. Mum's and Dad's generosity, workaholic attitude and ability to put everything before themselves has definitely rubbed off on me. I don't think I'm really that extravagant now, even though I most probably could be, but mostly I'm just grateful for how life has turned out. I'm lucky, aren't I? And I won't ever forget that. Every penny they had after bills would go on us two. Mum was a hairdresser and so she would take me with her to people's houses while she worked. I was born 18 months after my brother, so there wasn't a big age gap between us, and it must have been hard, but still she went back to work two days after I was born because she didn't want to let people down and because we needed the money – we'd just go with her and learn to be well-behaved!

I wanted to be a beautician from very early on. So Mum when she used to do all the old girls' hair, while she was doing the shampoo, set and perms, she'd ask them if they wanted their nails done. I had a little bag with some varnishes in, some files and some cuticle cream, and I loved it. They all had bunions and proper minging* feet. Oh my god, I'd file their feet and all that. They were all old girls and I'd be painting their nails bright green! They would give me a quid, sometimes two. I absolutely loved it and it kept me busy while mum did their hair.

We weren't with Dad as much during the week as Mum because Dad was in the fruit game – selling fruit and veg down the market, and then he moved into selling flowers, so he was off to work early, often before we even got up. It was tough for them but they did the best they could for us because they wanted us to have more than they did when they were growing up.

Dad had stalls on Romford Market and I'd spend hours there with him some Saturdays. I have happy memories of those times when me and my mum would go down and give him a hand on the weekend. It was a real family business in that sense. Having a good work ethic is key to success and has made a big difference to me and the way I see things – my parents instilled that in me from the beginning. It wasn't easy-come-easy-go, and although they wanted me and Billy to have everything, they never wanted us to take it for granted – we could see from one day to the next how hard it was for them. They compromised on everything so that we could have the best. Even down to our education. Billy and I went to private school – I don't know how they did it but they made it happen. Part of them sending us was so that we got the best education money could buy, but part of it was because Mum thought it was more secure. She wanted us to be safe all the time and she thought us going to a private school would be safer because they are generally smaller. In a way it sounds really over-the-top how Mum was with Billy and me, but it was something that is now just normal for both of us. I'd never go on the school trips because she didn't want us to go, scared that we would get lost or something. That's how bad Mum was at one point, she'd go: 'Instead of going, why don't I buy you a nice handbag?' and I was like: 'Alright then'. It was enough for me to be happy not to go on the trip. I didn't know anything else so it didn't bother me at all and I got a new handbag out of it! I mean, I was only young so it was just, like, a little handbag but it made me happy! Dad didn't say anything, I'm not sure if he even knew, but even if he did he would have been supportive because he knows why she's like she is. She's so worried about us, constantly, even now.

We didn't move house again after I was about eight, probably because they were trying to pay school fees! We rented in Hornchurch for about six to eight months, basically until Mum found the perfect house she liked in Brentwood – it was semi-detached and it was a really pretty house. I had a lovely bedroom and have happy memories of it, but we only stayed there for about six years until we found our next house in London Road, also in Brentwood. It was just around the corner and it was a lot bigger and detached. That's where I lived until I finally moved out two years ago. Mum couldn't believe it when I said I was ready to go. She was like: 'No way, Ames, you can't manage on your own.' In a way, she was right because she did everything for me and Billy, and I didn't even know how to turn the washing machine on. I'd been and stayed with my mate Jade (more about Jade later) for a week and I'd loved it. I liked having the independence and I knew it was the right time to go. I wasn't outgoing and so Mum was worried that I wouldn't cope. I found a really nice apartment in The Galleries in Brentwood and when the day came for me to move in Mum helped me. I couldn't believe I had my own place, but as she left she started to sob. She didn't want to leave me. She proper sobbed and I was like: 'Mum, it's just up the road from where you live. I'll be okay.' But, that was really hard for her. It was hard for me, too – I didn't know how to use an iron. I had to learn how to clean a bath, Mum had done everything for me so I wasn't independent at all and I had to learn quick. I stayed at The Galleries for six months and then I moved into where I am now – a chalet bungalow that I've totally gutted and done up. I love it round here and now I'm even closer to Mum's and Dad's house. They are just a few houses down from me – I'd hate to move too far away from them and I think Mum would hate it too, she likes to pop in and check up on me!

Mum and Dad still live in that house on London Road and they are really happy there and it's done up beautiful. They don't want anything fancy or in-your-face although Mum has always had a nice car and in the same way as she makes sure that Billy and me get everything, Dad does the same for her and wants her to have the nice things in life too. They are happy there, they have happy memories there of when me and Billy were kids growing up, and I still love that family home. I think they'll be there for a long time. They aren't flash people like that, they don't want some massive wag palace. Dad still drives around in a van because it's totally practical and he still works all the hours, and Mum has only recently stopped hairdressing all the time because she works so hard with my businesses, so she doesn't drive around in anything fancy either. If I ever showed signs of getting too big for my boots my parents would bring me back down to earth right away. They wouldn't let me mug anyone off*.

I loved my bedroom in Mum's and Dad's house, it had gorgeous wallpaper and when I was about ten I had curtains with lambs all over them put up and I loved them. I'm obsessed with animals and always have been. I had a beautiful, big double bed in the middle of the room – it was gorge and I loved it and so did all my friends, they were well jel and used to come 'round from school and go: 'I want Amy's bedroom!' I was very lucky. I tried to keep it tidy, but mostly Mum would come in after me and tidy up! As I've got older, though, I've got tidier and tidier, and now it's like I've got OCD! I flash-clean the kitchen every day! AND I have a cleaner once a week. I'm not even joking – I'm obsessed with cleanliness. Serious*.

Back to school, and my attempt at education! I have never found it easy. I am not academic and I'm severely dyslexic, so I needed a lot of extra help. I think Mum and Dad decided that by sending me privately I might be helped more and get further, because there were less kids in a class and more time could be spent with me. They sent me to Eastcourt Independent School in Goodmayes, Essex and it was one of the best schools in England. It's full of bright kids and I don't think I'd have got in but my dad's really good friend, Bernie, put in a good word for me and I managed to get a place. We didn't get any money off or anything but I wasn't the usual brainy kid, I was behind and I needed help every step of the way. Mum and Dad definitely went without to do that for us. We could have afforded to move into a better area and have better cars and holidays if it wasn't for the school fees but it was something they wanted to do for us, and both me and Billy are grateful for that. I left Eastcourt when I was 11 years old and then I went to Raphael Independent School in Romford. Sam and Billie Faiers were in the same class as me, although they left after a year because they didn't do senior private school and instead they went to Shenfield. Me and Sam have been mates ever since. I don't see either of them a lot, but when we are together we have a right laugh, proper banter and a great time. We have had some ups and downs since we were both on *TOWIE* but we are mates. I was upset by what Sam wrote in her book about me. She said that I put everything before my family and that really hurt because I am so close to them all and family is everything to me. It's lies and it was a really muggy* thing to say because I'd never do that. I'm not really sure why she said that but it's in the past now and it hasn't got in the way of us being mates. It's just one of those things and I think she regrets saying it.

Although I was very hard-working at school, I didn't love being there. I didn't hate it either but I always found it so hard. I always struggled. I couldn't really understand a lot of the things that the teachers were talking about and I'd switch off or go into my own little world – Amy's world! Parents' evenings were the worst because I'd always be at the bottom of the class every year. They were awful because what could they say about me? I was doing badly, I was never doing well. Apart from me having good manners and being very polite and never getting into trouble, there weren't any positives. I was good, but I wasn't clever. School reports were the same too – they were horrific. So bad. My dad would just say to me: 'Ames, don't worry babe – there's only one way to go when you are at the bottom and that's up', which was such a sweet thing for him to say and his encouragement would help my confidence. Dad never really went to school much himself and Mum says she never learned a thing where she went to school in the East End of London. Their main thing was that they wanted to try and give us the best. The fact that we were polite, nice and well-mannered was all my parents wanted to hear, although I used to try and explain why it was a bad report! But honestly they didn't worry about it. Dad would say to me: 'You're the most beautiful child ever in the world.' He was proud of me, no matter what.

Being at the bottom did affect my confidence, but the school was really good at helping to get the best out of me even if it wasn't in academic areas, like public speaking, and because of my family I didn't let it knock me. They'd get me to focus on my strengths and Dad was right, if you are at the bottom, there is only one way to go. It's true and look at where I am now…

Both Mum and Dad just wanted me to try my best and they said that was all they could ever ask for, they didn't care if I got an F or a G as long as it was my best effort. 'Always try, always try' they'd say...

We found out that I was dyslexic when I was four years old. I'd be told something and then a day later I'd forget what I'd been told – I couldn't hold on to anything in my head for very long. I was tested to see how bad it was – they tested me in Maths and English, and then gave Mum and Dad a report on what they had found. It said that my dyslexia was severe, so I got extra time in exams and things like that if I needed it.

I just found it really hard at school and that put me off going sometimes. It was hard when all my friends seemed to be really clever and I'd be saying to myself: 'How are they so good at this? How do they understand it and I don't?' It mugged me right off. I was known at school for being the thick one but I was quite strong and it never really upset me... well, some bits did, but it was more of a banter thing in the end, you know. There were times when we had tests and people would ask each others' scores and it would be like: 'What you got Amy? Zero?' Stuff like that was horrible, it wasn't bullying, it was just banter, but it wasn't nice. I suppose it gave me thicker skin in a way because at times I do need it now – just look at my Twitter feed some days. LOL.

It was so bad that Mum and Dad used to get me extra private tuition after school. I hated it. I preferred to be doing my own thing, not sat there listening to another teacher! The doorbell would go and I'd be like: 'I can't stand it. I don't wanna have a lesson.' I'd really moan about it and then Bob, who was the teacher, would walk in and I'd be asking him if he wanted an Earl Grey tea! So I'd be giving Mum all this jip* and the minute the teacher walked in I'd be nice and all that. I was really bad at Science and Bob was trying to help me but, according to Mum, I moaned and moaned about him coming over. I never did do well in Science, I just couldn't take the information in. But even though I hated those lessons, I was still polite!

The thing is, and I don't know how to say this without sounding big-headed, I wasn't a bad-looking kid and the boys wanted to go out with me. I was the thick one but they fancied me, you know. Funny. Sometimes people saying stuff hurt me, of course it did, and I would go home and tell Mum about what had been said. I remember asking my mum why I wasn't like this girl in my class; she was really brainy and I wanted to be like her. And Mum said to me: 'Ames, you don't wanna be rude like her and a bully like her. I bet she'd like to be as pretty as you.' That was Mum's way of making me feel better and it worked. On the days that it got me down I'd think about that. But in a way I've come back and I've fought harder for everything because I had to. Good things in life don't come easy, that's for sure. I've always tried my hardest, even at school, from when I was five to when I was 16, I always tried. I always did my homework. I wasn't a bad girl, you know. Of course, we're all lazy at times but I tried my best no matter. In the end I got Ds, Es and Fs, but I got a B in French. How random is that? I don't know how that happened. I surprised myself with that one because it was out of the ordinary for me to do well. Even with the small classes at private school, I couldn't do well. In my Geography class there were just three of us and I still got an F. I felt a bit bad to be honest because I was thinking; 'all that money Mum and Dad are spending and I'm still failing.' I think about that sometimes, but you know what? I'd do the same for my kids – I'd send them to private school, for sure. It helped me to get a confidence that I'm not sure I'd have had otherwise and I felt protected in a way.

When I was about nine years old I was sent for elocution lessons. I'm serious. It makes me laugh as soon as I think about it! I can even speak posh when I want to but it just ain't me. I'm from Essex and I speak like someone from Essex (yes, please do ignore my bad grammar) but in those classes they'd teach us to pronounce all our words proper. Making us put 'Ts' on the ends of words and making sure we didn't drop sounds. I swear on my life I had elocution lessons and I did it for a couple of years, but then I decided I didn't like speaking like that so I went back to how I speak now. A waste of time and money, I know!

At the time I was in class with a lot of clever people who all spoke posh. All their dads were city brokers, they had loads of money and then there was me, you know, my dad's a market trader ('Alright darling, how's it going?') so I was around people that were different to me and my family and suddenly I had to try and speak like them, all posh. I ended up speaking really posh for a while. It was weird.

There was about 45 of us doing these lessons and we all had to get a distinction. I'm sure that was it and we had to get one to pass the whole thing. We had to get up and talk to everyone about whatever we wanted but we had to really, you know, pronounce all the words properly while we were doing it. I went up and talked about beauty and I nailed it. People were talking about football or cricket or gymnastics, but I spoke about my passion and I don't think they could believe it. Suddenly I came into my own and I surprised them all. I got hand cream, I got a nail file and I got nail polish and I went through the process of having, like, a manicure, and I beat everyone. I was the highest in the class and I got the distinction. It was a massive confidence boost for me. I got 98%. Someone was coming in to assess us, and I was on 98%. Never in my life had I got over, like, 10% or something like that so it was a massive deal. The guy who was assessing us was shocked as well. It was a turning point for me because it was like: I've done something that I'm so proud of. I loved the feeling of doing something well, it was my first taste of success in a way, and I can remember it like it was yesterday. I was so, so proud that I wanted to cry. When I went home I couldn't wait to tell Mum and Dad. And that was that, it changed my whole view of everything. I had found something I could do really well. In my head, I'd moved forward. The headmaster, Mr Malitscar, obviously knew I was severely dyslexic but he sat me down and I'll tell you what he said to me… 'You will be successful Amy. You will be, Amy. You will be a very successful businesswoman.' I was shocked. It meant the world to me and I had proved something to myself as well as the school.

I think that's the point I'm trying to make – everyone is good at something and although I wasn't intelligent, I was social and able to walk into rooms full of people and speak about the things I love, which a lot of the brainy lot couldn't handle. Make the most of what you've got. I have with my personality.

I suppose it's only to be expected, but I have lost friends along the way. I still speak to a lot of my old mates, but some find what I'm doing now a bit weird, I think. I find that hard because I know that I haven't changed but they must feel uneasy about it all. I can't stand all that agg between people and I'd rather walk away. I know I'm the same person. One of my really good school friends I saw out at the shops one day after I'd started in *TOWIE*. I was so close to her at school and when she saw me she didn't say a thing to me, I was quite hurt by it. I don't understand why people would be different with me. Mum says that maybe it's jealousy? I know one of my mates totally cut me out when I started to get endorsements. Overnight it seemed like she hated me and stopped speaking to me. I don't know. I don't get it. I don't see how best friends can be really jealous of you or why they would think we can't still be friends just because I'm famous now. People change drastically and it makes me cynical and I hate that because I'm a happy and positive person. These sort of things are the downside to all this. True friends will always stand by you and I've definitely found out who my real friends are, and my family haven't changed towards me at all, probably because

I haven't changed from the girl who used to live with them. They still treat me as Ames, their daughter and sister.

I never thought I'd be famous – people might have said it to me but I never believed it. I just wanted to work in a salon doing what I loved, I never thought beyond that. Everyone that met me did, though. They said: 'Amy's got something'. I don't know what that was but they said it was a sparky thing, a character that people always wanted to be around. I was never the loud one, I was actually quite quiet, not like Billie and Sam – they were the girls, proper girls and I was the goody two-shoes!

With all the name-calling and that, I'd try and focus on the fact that I was the glam one. I might be thick but I'm glam! I've always tried to look my best. Claire, my manager, says that I'm like a young Joan Collins! But I like to look nice – I'd never go out without doing my make-up. I was immaculate at school and I did my hair every day. I'd be told off for wearing make-up because that was against the rules, but I did it anyway! Mum wasn't a strict mum but she'd have a go at me if I did my make-up badly and when I had that massive line from the foundation along my jaw! I thought I was well cool. My school was well strict and Mum got called in a few times because I was wearing mascara but I couldn't go in without it, could I?! Sam and Billie would also wear make-up to school but the teachers were having none of it!

Despite not going to a school that let me wear make-up, I am well lucky and I know that because me and Billy had such a loving upbringing. My parents are still together which is quite unusual really, as a lot of my mates' parents have broken up, but Mum and Dad are totally still in love. I have never heard them really argue or get annoyed with each other, they just seem to work and I hope that when I am their age me and my husband will love and care for each other as much as they do. My dad adores my mum and he tells her every day that he loves her – they are a little unit and that makes me happy. They've been together for, like, 30 years; they are best friends and you don't often see that. I enjoy that. I'm proud that my parents are still together and happy.

Family means everything to me. My dad's nan, my great-nan (Nanny Joan), lived with us in Manor Park and all I remember was my mum cooking with her. She would always cook and help my mum out. Because Mum was working full-time, Nanny Joan would do a lot of the things at home with us, like getting our tea. She loved Billy and me like we were her own kids, and when she passed away on 21st April 2012 I was devastated. That was the first time I had felt pain like it and it was really hard. She left a massive gap in all of our lives because she taught me so much. I might not be the brightest, brainiest person, but I am kind and loving and hard-working – all things she and my parents have taught me to be, and that influence is definitely part of the key to me being successful and why I think I've stayed around as long as I have since leaving *TOWIE*.

I've got a big family – Mum is one of four. Her older sister is called Jackie and she has got nine kids! Mum is probably closest to her youngest sister, my Auntie Karen, who is Harry

(Derbidge)'s mum. Harry and I are so similar and I've been with him since the day he was born. I am so protective of him. He's got an amazing personality and we are like brother and sister in a lot of ways. We argue like siblings but we couldn't be without each other. He's always the one who tells me exactly what he thinks and has a go at my boyfriends. I trust Harry's opinions more than anyone's and we have always been so close. I've been close to his brother Ronnie too, but Harry was like my live dolly when I was little and I always wanted to be with him. That's why I got Harry on the show, I hated being a part of something that he wasn't and it was brilliant when he did get a part. The thing I love about Harry is that he's so funny. He's always been like he is now – a bit feminine and he always preferred the girls' toys rather than the boys' ones! I knew from the minute he was born that he was gay. I just knew it. I've got amazing memories of Harry from when we were little, unbelievable memories! I remember us going to McDonald's one time, he would go a bit shy and nervous because he wanted a girl's toy instead of a boy's toy in the Happy Meal! I want to talk about my honey Harry a lot in this book – he means the world to me and since *TOWIE* he has started his own business and been really successful with it. He deserves his success because he works so hard. He's such a brilliant person and I just want the best for him and for him to be successful – and for him to meet Mr Right! 😉 I never in a million years thought I could do what I've gone and done and achieved, and I wish Harry could do the same. He deserves it.

Family holidays were the best, and Harry and Ronnie and Auntie Karen and Nanny Joan would come along too. We went to Potters (Potters Leisure Resort in Hopton-on-Sea) a few times. Nanny Joan would always come to Butlins with us and I've got some amazing, amazing pictures of me and my brother on holiday. I look at them and they make me smile. We were so innocent! My mum loved her fashion but some of it was out of order! I went through a right chubby stage, too – I suppose everyone does, but I look back now and those pictures are well cringe*. In every picture you can see me with my pink blanket. I loved that blanket and it came everywhere with me. I'm still obsessed with it and I take it to bed with me even now, although I do wash it every week! I lost it on holiday at Butlins once. It was like my world had ended! We found it in the end, thank God, but if they hadn't found it I probably wouldn't have slept all that holiday. Ever since I was little I had things that I became attached to and couldn't bear to part with. Mum used to dress us in really good clothes. She'd spend a lot of money on pretty dresses for me, even if it meant going without herself. I always looked like I was going to a party – that's probably why I'm like I am!

We used to have a wicked time on holiday, some of my happiest memories are at Potters or down the caravan with Nanny Joan. Some summers we'd go to Portugal and one year we went to Cyprus and then after that we started to go to Madeira, so we were lucky that we did have those lovely holidays. Again, everyone would come along. The first time we went to Portugal Harry was in a buggy and I spent the whole holiday pushing him around. I loved it. I was obsessed with Harry. He is my best friend. Yeah, he drives me mad a lot and we argue all the time, but I love him so much. And the same way as I was obsessed with him, he was obsessed with me! Growing up we were pretty inseparable. I think because we are such a close family it's not that surprising really and most weekends we'd all be together, in and out of the house.

Mum loved Madeira and we went to the same place for seven years on the trot. Sounds odd, but Mum didn't want to go to a place where there were too many other kids because then she knew that there would be them kids' clubs and she didn't want us going to those. She would never let us go to anything like that and Dad used to tease her that we needed to go to a Robinson Crusoe island where it was just us! Mum actually would have liked that. They were great holidays and we made lots of friends while we were there. The holidays were all about family – me, Billy and Harry having a good time. But when it came to the evening it was 'grown-up' time. I always remember Mum being like: 'Ames, Billy, Harry – it's grown-up time at night. It's been all about you today and now it's our time.' It was fair enough really. We'd go out for dinner but we'd be quiet and behave. We'd play on our computers or draw or something but we knew that we had to be quiet. That was the deal.

Christmases are huge for us. One year we went to Bury St Edmonds, which was really nice and I really enjoyed it, but Mum hated it because she loves having a big Christmas at home. She loves having a load of people in the house, bustling about, so now we either have everyone to us or we go to Auntie Karen's. Christmas is one of my favourite times of the year; everyone is round the house and happy, and even now, for me, it's one of the few days that I feel like I have off. I know that sounds stupid but since being in the public eye every day feels like a work-day. I'm not moaning, I love it, but on Christmas Day it's like a proper day off! It's the small things… Dad always does the tree, my mum never gets involved in all of that and then when he's finished we all come in to see it. It's never a real tree, always a fake so that it's perfect and there's not a mess! It's crazy, really, if you come to think about it, as my dad sells Christmas trees on the market, but my mum wants a fake one so she gets a fake one!

My family unit has taught me how important relationships are, whether it's in business or in my personal life. I've been successful but I'm not prepared to tread on people to get to the top – that's just not me. I want to be able to sleep at night and be liked. If that makes it harder for me to get to the top then that's the way it is. You won't see me kicking ass; it ain't my style.

I know what's wrong and right, but I'm not one of these people that shouts about things. I'm pretty laidback, as it goes, but I wouldn't want anyone to think they could mug me off because of that. Like with the salon – I know what I want and how I want it to be, and I won't take any excuses but there's no need to shout to get my point across. I look at

Mum and Dad as my role models; they are workaholics and I am too. I'm never lazy and I always do what I say I'll do. If I need to be somewhere, I am there... I never go back on my word and that's important in business. Really important. For me being honest and trustworthy is a big positive and that's what my parents are, and look how well they've done. They might not be mega rich but they've done better and better every year through hard work and determination. Nothing comes easily in life and if you don't work, you can't expect to better yourself or make money or whatever your motivation might be to succeed. Hard graft is the key. Mum's the same as Dad when it comes to knuckling down and getting a job done; she's never been work-shy and even now she never stops working. My family are unbelievable, everyone that meets them always falls in love with Mum and Dad. My dad is funny, he's the funniest person ever and when he's in the room everyone laughs. He's a real person, he loves banter, he takes the piss out of people, but in a funny way. He might have done well for himself but he doesn't care because no amount of money or fame would alter my dad; he will never change and that's the beauty of him. And that's why I love my family so much.

I don't know how many people believe in star signs but I do. I'm a Gemini and I definitely have two sides; I think I've got a business head that kicks in when I'm at work, when I have to deal with conflict or difficult decisions, and then there's the other Amy, my twin, who is the real me. The Amy that likes to be at home, being the family one and spending time with friends – watching movies, drinking prosecco and munching on Twiglets.

Yeah, I see Amy Childs 'the businesswoman' and then I see Amy Childs 'the girl in a onesie watching a film on the sofa'. I've come a long way in these last few years and I've had to grow up big-time. Sometimes I'm not sure that's a good thing because underneath it all, underneath the success and happy bank balance, is Amy Childs – a really young girl who's really fun, you know. They are very different people and, I'm not going to lie, I find that hard at times. I get the hump* about it sometimes. It's weird because on the one hand I'm totally happy with everything, but on the other I struggle with the pressures. I think that's probably normal and why anyone who is anyone needs good people around them, keeping their feet on the ground and making sure that it all doesn't become too much. Some days it does. I'm sure even Victoria Beckham gets days like that when she wishes she could walk away from it all and lead a normal life. I started all of this when I was 19, when most girls are getting boyfriends and going out. I haven't really done any of those normal teenage things. When I started *TOWIE* my life changed forever. I'm not complaining about that but I'd be lying if I said there weren't times that I didn't or don't enjoy the idea of being able to be just me some days or be the 24-year-old that I actually am. Everyone thinks I am older, but it's because I've had to fast-track growing up. Some of those years that people get their childishness out of their system have been lost for me. With a pap\* lens in your mug every time you move, it's not always easy to let your hair down, is it?

Maybe everyone thinking I'm a lot older just comes from the industry that I work in. Like I said, you can't just go out and go to a club and get drunk and fall out (as in be blind drunk and held up by one of your mates), and have no one notice. That won't happen if you are Amy Childs! LOL. I can't do that, because if I did I'd be tarnished in a way. I have my guard up when I'm out and that's why I definitely prefer a night in with my mates, like a barbecue or something. Hannah, the manager of my salon, gets so annoyed with me never wanting to go out that she says she's designing my garden so that the party can come to me. I'm a home-bod... what can I say?!

Mum and Dad might have been very loving and generous, but they were bloody hard on us. So, so strict. Like, a good strict, but I guess in a way I was scared of my dad because when he told us off, he really told us off. I remember one time when dad went totally mad. My mum used to take us round to some of her clients' houses sometimes when she didn't have anyone to look after us and she expected us to sit there and behave. We could read or whatever but we were told to be on our best behaviour. It was Mum's work, and we knew that and we knew we must do as we were told. That's how it was. So, I remember going round there, to this lady's house, she was called Nelly, and me and Billy was fighting. It was only a little fight but I started crying and as I turned around in a complete state I knocked these ornaments over.

Nelly's ornaments were all amazing and my mum went off the planet. She was mad, mad, MAD. I was only about seven or eight but I knew we was gonna cop it.

I was definitely a late-developer, I was obsessed with babies, as in toy dolls, and if you wanted to punish me then stopping me from having Baby Matthew was the way to get to me, big-time. Baby Matthew was my favourite. My mum has still got him at her house even now! I'd hate it if he got thrown out, I loved that baby! He's upstairs in his Silver Cross pram, yeah! When I was 14 I used to take Baby Matthew with me when I went out. It was about that age when I started to experiment with make-up and that, and I would put on a little bit of clear mascara. I always had men look at me, it was weird. People would go: 'oh my god, is he your baby?' They'd think I was older and had a baby! I just used to go along with it for a laugh and not to look like a mug. They would go to my dad, if it was him that was with me and say: 'I thought she had a real baby!' I was looking really glam, walking along with a baby in a Silver Cross pram! I used to go to the airport with a big ponytail in and wear a little top, which had the words 'fit' on it, and then have Baby Matthew in the pram – even then people thought I was older!

I loved Barbie, but loved that doll more. Yeah, and I used to meet up with my friend Claud and she used to be a baby-lover as well, so we would always have our two babies sitting there wherever we were. It got to a point where I felt a bit of peer pressure not to be playing with the babies anymore and, yeah, sometimes I felt a bit embarrassed and I'd ask my mum not to tell people that I still played with him, but I loved Matthew. He had beautiful little slacks on and everything, and my mum used to go Sainsbury's and I would go: 'Can you pick up some nappies for Matthew?' and then she'd come home with them and give Matthew a little cuddle. He was one of the family!

I used to take him everywhere and, like, he would have all the best outfits. He would have baby grows, proper baby grows and everything. At that time he was my life, like, he had a cot next to my bed and even when I was 14 years old he came on holiday with me. See what I mean about being a late developer? That's a bit scary to admit in a book isn't it?! I'll probably get trolled for that now! Anyways, going back to the story… so I had Baby Matthew and me and Billy, and we was really naughty and smashed the ornaments. Nelly was so sweet she kept saying: 'Don't worry, it doesn't matter.' But, it mattered. Believe me, it mattered. This was for real and Mum was gonna do one on us! So that night my dad found out. I knew it was coming as soon as he got home. My dad ran upstairs and really told me off and got Baby Matthew and threw him down the stairs. Baby Matthew used to have a thing where if you moved his arm, it moved his eyes, but his eyes didn't work anymore after Dad had chucked him down the stairs. I remember that like it was yesterday. I've never sobbed so much, ever, in my life, because Baby Matthew was destroyed, he was never the same again and honestly I didn't know what to do with myself. We couldn't get him fixed, but I learned to love him even more. Dad felt so bad and was like: 'I shouldn't have done that to Baby Matthew. I'm sorry.' He was really upset by it and it ended up with me and Dad crying together.

You see, Dad is the best dad any girl could ask for. But he didn't take any nonsense and was hard on us because he didn't want us to grow up being brats or not having manners. Manners are a big deal to both Mum and Dad.

Billy and me would always argue like any brother or sister but there are certain rucks that were 'OMG' rucks. One time we were arguing in the car over some toys we were playing with. We were going on and on, and my dad was getting more and more annoyed with us. The next thing we knew he'd got hold of the toys, wound the window down and chucked them out. We both just sat there in the back of the car, shocked. One minute we were arguing over some toys and the next they were gone forever. 'Forever' because he never went back to get them. That was our punishment for behaving so badly! Harsh, wasn't it? He tries to be hard on us these days but it's difficult now I'm older and have moved out. I think the last time he got proper stressed-out with me was when I had my boobs done. He wasn't impressed.

The thing is with Dad, he'd be mad one minute and the next he'd have forgotten about it. For some reason he used to think that because Mum was a hairdresser that I could easily cut his hair too, but he found out the hard way that this wasn't true. Mum went to pick up Billy from table-tennis one time and he asked me to get the clippers and give him a skinhead. I knew it couldn't be too hard to do, so I thought:

'Why not, this is brilliant. I'll give it a go!' So I did. I put one of those grading attachments on the clippers and started to shave his head but all of a sudden the attachment popped off and it left a massive bald spot. Literally, a bald spot, right there on his head! I couldn't stop laughing, I thought it was hilarious and then when Mum came back I burst out crying because I knew she'd be proper mad with me. He looked like some kind of bouncer doorman, you know? It was so hilarious but Mum didn't think it was that funny! Mum tried to sort it out but there was a shorter bit for quite a while. I think Dad saw the funny side. After all, it was him who'd asked me to cut his hair and I'm not actually a hairdresser!

## CHAPTER 2

# IT'S ALL ABOUT THE GLAMOUR...

Glam is my thing. It's in me and I've always been the same. Whether it was walking to Tesco with my mum as a kid or going to a party, I always looked the same – as in, my make-up was flawless and my hair was done. These days I'll nip to the supermarket with my rollers in but no one looks twice, that's normal 'round here. But I'd never walk out looking like a mess. I couldn't do it. It's not just something that I became interested in as I got older... even as a young girl I loved dressing up. Back then, it was in my mum's shoes – power dressing from an early age! I'd pinch her make-up bag and do God-knows-what to my face. One of my favourite games was to play 'holidays', which involved dressing up as if we were going away. Mum hated me playing that game because it made a total mess. Me and my friends or me and my brother would get all our wardrobe out, put everything in a suitcase and literally just walk up the stairs with it all. We would pretend that the stairs were the aeroplane. When we got back to the room the game was over and that was that. Total carnage. Every time people came over I'd try and play that game, and Mum would beg me not to! It's funny, because I was so into dressing up, I'd like to dress other people up to.

One time Harry was over (we weren't that old, probably about ten) and Harry asked me to do his hair and I thought: 'I'm going to dress him up. Amaze*.' By the time I'd finished, Harry had my little sparkly dress on from Tammy Girl, some of my mum's heels and a heap of make-up. We went downstairs and went: 'TA-DAH'. Everyone was like 'Oh my god' 'cause he looked so good! He looked like a pretty little girl. Seriously, he looked good. Dressing up was just a bit of fun but he looked amazing, no one knew whether to clap or what. They were in shock. After that we'd do it all the time and we'd put on shows at, like, family dos. We'd do a bit of dancing and we were always the Spice Girls. I was always Emma Bunton. I loved Baby Spice and Harry was always happy to play along.

Looking back, Mum let me be pretty glam all the time. There were a few parts of my childhood that weren't quite so exciting, like the homework, which Mum and Dad would make me sit down and do. I'd just stare out of the window or brush my hair. I found it so hard to concentrate on anything like that but they made me do it. Dad couldn't really help because he didn't have a clue either, so I struggled on getting terrible grades!

The other thing was table-tennis. Me and Billy were part of a team. Billy was the one who got us into it and I find it a bit weird now when I think about it but it kept me busy and it was harmless fun. Billy used to play every Friday night, so Mum used to drop me off with him and all of a sudden I decided I wanted to play. My mum was like: 'You're gonna play table-tennis?' and I was like: 'Yeah I'm gonna give it a go.'

I like to do random things sometimes and surprise people. I think I surprise people quite a lot. Billy would be playing his tournaments and then they'd let me have a go and teach me how to play. One of the coaches said to me, sounding quite surprised, 'you're really good, you've got an amazing backhand and forehand.' That was it, that started me playing table-tennis and I played three times a week and had my own session with a coach. Crazy.

I was always very young for my age and by that point there was no way that a lot of my friends would be going to play table-tennis, and in a way I think my mum liked that. She liked that I was doing something sensible. I think 'sensible' is the right word for me in a lot of ways because I've never been the crazy kid hanging out in places I shouldn't. My mum wouldn't have that. No way.

I was always with my mum. I always wanted to be with her. As I got older and I started to get invited to parties after school I wouldn't want to go because I started to worry that Mum might not pick me up, so I'd decide that I didn't want to go. I would go: 'Mum, you have to come with me, I don't want to go on my own.' Of course, she was going to pick me up but I started to worry and panic about it because, other than being at school, me and Billy were always with her. So I never used to go to parties.

I don't know how it all started and why I started to feel like that but, in a way, I missed out on quite a bit because I wouldn't be without her at any time. Just to explain things a bit and to explain why Mum is as protective as she is… my mum was left as a child. She was only three years old when her mum left them all – and that's been really tough on Mum, as you can imagine. I can't picture being without a mum so it must have been awful for her.

My mum had the worst upbringing. It's unbelievable what she went through, unbelievable. She has told Billy and me all about it and, like I say, I think it made her doubly protective of us. You remember I mentioned the holidays to Madeira? Well, that's why she would never let us in the holiday clubs. That's why she'd have preferred a Robinson Crusoe island. She always wanted us with her; she barely let us out of her sight really. If you ask Mum now, she'll tell you that we weren't allowed out of her sight until we were 16. Being left like that at such a young age means that Mum has got major issues when it comes to our safety and making sure that we are protected and looked after. Even at 16, it was hard for her to do but she knew she had to let us out. We needed to be a bit street-wise. When she was at school she says she was fighting every day and she didn't want anything like that for us. She wrapped us in cotton wool really because, me and Billy, we are Mum's and Dad's life and world.

All she wanted was to make sure we were safe all the time and that no one could hurt us. Because I love Mum so much, I always worried for her and also I wanted to be with her. So if I did ever go to a party, I wouldn't really enjoy myself and I would wonder what time Mum was picking me up. Sleepovers were totally out of the question. There's no way I could have done that because I felt so homesick. Even at, like, 12 or 13 I hated being away from Mum and home. Sam and Billie's mum, Sue, was one of the very few people that Mum totally trusted. My mum and dad love Sue, and Sue got how my mum was with us. She understood. Sue would be like: 'Don't worry, Julie, I've got Amy in bed and we're having a cuddle.' Mum knew we were safe with her and being loved. I'd go round Sam's house to stay over and by the time it came for us to go to bed I'd start to cry. Every time I'd say: 'Sue can you get Mum to pick me up please?'

Now I don't live at home anymore, but Mum's only a few doors down and she'll pop in all of the time. I always text her before I go to bed to let her know that I'm safe and I'm at home. Even if we row and stop talking I'll always do that because I know she'd be well worried if I didn't and she wouldn't sleep. What can I say? She's a very protective mum. Sam and Billie would be out and about on a Friday night but Mum would never let me. I think she was worried that I might get hurt. She was worried that I wouldn't come home.

Being at home a lot meant that I had a lot of time to get on and do things! I loved reading and that was a bit of an escape for me. I loved, loved reading. Jacqueline Wilson – I read all of her books. I read all the Roald Dahl books. I was a big readaholic. Like, I actually loved a book. It's weird, isn't it? I am dyslexic and not great at school but there I was reading all of the time. I'm that sort of person – I want to achieve and I believe you can if you try hard enough. I've always tried my best, no matter what it's been. Because Mum and Dad are so hot on manners, I think that if they'd had a choice over whether we were brainy or well-mannered they'd have taken the manners every time. Lucky, eh?! Even now Mum will pull me up if I forget to say 'please' or 'thank you'! In a way, I was the perfect child! I was really good for Mum and it was really late on in my teens when I started to try and push it a bit, but even then I wasn't that bad. I'd just put a bit too much make-up on or something. Nothing bad.

Mum's never liked my boyfriends, but maybe that's just normal for mums and their daughters' blokes. I do go for bad boys, that's for sure. I can't see myself settling down with some city sort. Nah, that isn't me. I like a bit of a bad boy. We all do round here… I think that's the Essex in us! I can't help it, that's just the way I am. That's probably the only thing I'm not that sensible over. I do wear my heart on my sleeve and I'm easily used, I know that and fame has made that harder.

My first boyfriend was lovely… he was called Billy Smith and he was my first love. I still love him now, he was a right sort and everyone wanted to get off* with him! He was a bit of a weapon*. Billy was the love of my life – he really was. I suppose everyone thinks that about their first boyfriend.

I met him because he was working at our house. Mum had to have her front drive done, and when she told me I asked her whether she was getting these lads in – Billy and his two brothers. So, they're three brothers – Dan, James and Billy (the youngest) – and they're all good-looking. Once they were working on the house, everyone, even my mum's mates, were over to have a good look at them! They were all unbelievable. I went to Mum: 'Oh my god, I really like Billy.' She's like: 'God, Ames, he's twenty-one and you're fifteen, you're at school.' But whenever Billy was 'round I'd be in a bit of a fluster, put my make-up and little shorts on, and make myself look good. I had blonder hair at the time, and I'd go and ask the boys if they wanted a cup of tea! Any excuse to speak to him! I was like: 'I'd love to be with him and have a little bit of a flirt-up on text', but every girl fancied him; he was the boy to be with in Brentwood.

One day I got myself all dressed up and took the teas out. It was a hot day so I had tiny shorts on and I put some sandals on and said I was going to walk up to Brentwood High Street. He offered me a lift but I said 'Nah', I'd walk. I asked them if they wanted anything because I was trying to get their attention and Billy said he wanted some chocolate. So muggy me picked him up some chocolates! While I was walking to the shops, my phone buzzed and he'd text me to remind me to pick up the chocolate and I was like: 'He's text me! He's actually texting me.' That's how it started and we were together for a year. Mum and Dad really liked him. In fact, they absolutely loved him. We went to Greece together, our first holiday, when I was 16 and he was 21. He was just, like, unbelievable. Everyone was so jealous of me and because he was older it was even more cool. He used to tell me he loved me all the time and all that. All the messages were so sweet, like: 'You look beautiful today, can't wait to cuddle you.' He was a lovely boy. He had a brand new car and there I was still at school doing my GCSEs! We broke up because of the age difference – I was too young for him and it didn't work. He ended it with me and said he just couldn't do it anymore because he felt I was quite young. I was distraught because I had fallen in love with him and I didn't get over him for a long time; I think it took me about two years. I still see him around all the time – he's not married or anything and he text me not so long ago and was like: 'Are you alright, Ame?' I didn't text him back, although he's, like, a mate now, but at the time, when you're younger, it's like your world is ended.

Besides, I'm with Brad now and I'm happy. I met him at the pub and it took us a while to go public because I wanted to see where it was going. As soon as I say I'm with someone there's a load of pressure on the relationship, and I didn't want that. He's a proper sort and he's decent. He doesn't use me for fame or money, he's not interested at all and that on it's own makes me happy. I always worry that people might be with me for the wrong reasons, but not with Brad – he ain't bothered by all that. When I first started on *TOWIE*, local boys would chat me up because I was on the TV. I knew why they were suddenly interested and that was something

I had to deal with. Who wants to be with someone because they are on TV? Too many people and that's horrible. It's the dark side to fame that no one ever sees until they are in that position. Obviously there are huge positives to all this and on the one hand I was having a great time. I'm not going to lie, the attention was amazing and all that, and I was starting to make good money. I was having a bloody ball – I was going to the National Television Awards and I was suddenly finding myself at Peter Andre's house with him asking me if I wanted a coffee. That was so surreal. Mum was with me and Mum was like: 'Can you believe that we are in Peter Andre's house?' We were pissing ourselves – his kids were there and it was mental. We stayed there until about 2am that night and Mum had to go to Dagenham the next morning to do some old girl's hair. One minute she's sitting in Pete's house and the next she's back doing her regular job. Mad.

It felt like I was hitting the big time but the idea that people were starting to hang around me because of it didn't sit easy with me. Not at all. Boys chatting me up and all that, when really all they wanted was to get on the show themselves.

That's one of the hardest things about being in the press – you never really know if people are with you for the right reasons. That's definitely a downside to all of this and something I find really tough. How can you ever really know? You can only hope.

I do have a bit of a habit of going for the wrong sort of bloke but these days my main criteria is that they don't care what I do. They need to look nice too, obvs. Mum is never keen on my boyfriends but I think my boyfriend choice is me rebelling in a funny way, if you know what I mean. Apart from the surgery, which wasn't even that rebellious, I've never done that off-the-rails thing. I never got any tattoos. I just don't like them. Can you imagine on your wedding day having a big sleeve of tats? Not ladylike at all. I also think in business it doesn't look great. First impressions do count when you meet people and, for me, I think they are disgusting. 100%.

The worst I ever had was a tongue piercing. You probably remember me having it on *TOWIE*. I haven't got it in now but tried it again the other day randomly. I found the bar, so I put it in and the hole hasn't closed up, it still went through, but it slows my speech down. When I was on *TOWIE* there's a few scenes where I've got the bar in and I sound a bit different. I had to take it out in the end because it was hard to understand me! I never got anything else pierced, I don't think... except for my belly button, but that's well old-school. I had two in my belly button when I was younger – I was 13 when I had those done! Oh, and my ears but I only had them done once. I never went in for a load of piercings in my ears. Nah. See, I was pretty good like that and I wasn't a massive party animal – going out drinking and all that. Mum's never picked me up off the floor proper paralytic drunk (FYI: I have been pretty drunk but it's rare and not in front of Mum!) and I've never taken drugs, and I think me liking the bad boys is *that* part of me that likes to kick back a bit and not do as I'm told all the time! I can remember being spectacularly drunk the night before one of my driving lessons. Actually, it was my first driving lesson and I'd gone out the night before so I felt rough. As soon as I got in the car he asked me what I'd been doing the night before and I told him that I'd been out drinking and he went: 'You shouldn't be driving then', and then we had some good banter* but I got myself into such a kerfuffle that he didn't end up letting me drive. But anyway, I had a great relationship with this guy. I remember one of the lessons where he'd taken me out, he said: 'Look to your right', but I'd misheard him and I'd thought he'd said: 'You look alright.' So I was like: 'Are you joking? I'm wearing a track suit.' It was so awful because the minute I said it I realised that he hadn't said what I thought he had. I nearly died of embarrassment. From that day on we just really clicked. It was proper funny.

The time for going right off the rails has kind of passed me by, although there are days when I think I'm going to just do it and rebel BIG time! But being happy is the most important thing, and I am.

I'm not a massive party girl, like I said. Yeah, I like to go out now and again but, for me, I like curling up with Brad and watching a film or something and he likes that too. We suit each other in that way. He likes me because I'm 'Ames' not 'Amy Childs off *TOWIE*' and that means a lot. He pays his way and he expects nothing from me. He hasn't got some fancy job in the city but he works hard and he's grown up a lot. Brad has a little girl from a previous relationship and she is gorgeous. It makes me proper broody at times. I am a big family person and – even with all the amazing stuff, and it is amazing, that I get to do – my happiest moments are at home with the people I love. A lot of my friends have started to settle down and have babies and there's a part of me that really aches for that, but I have a lot to do before I go down that road. Although, if it happens, it happens. I believe in fate and what will be, will be. There's nothing I want more, and I do believe that women can have a career and be a mum, but there's quite a bit more I want to achieve first if I can. I'm only 25 remember, so there's still time! You can never predict what's around the corner and I'd never sacrifice a family for my career but I'm lucky that even if I had a baby now I'm financially secure and I'd think of a way of adapting what I do. Everything is possible if you want it to be and you believe in it.

Apart from blokes, I think I'm generally pretty sensible and have my head screwed on. I have respect for my parents and, even now, if something comes out in the press about me I worry about what Mum will think. She's an amazing person and I don't want to hurt her, particularly because I feel bad for the way she was brought up. I look at my mum and think my mum is my life and she had nobody. All she did was look after Karen and Jackie, her sisters, and that's why she panics about everything and that's why she doesn't really like any of my blokes. I just want to make her happy and proud and that drives me to do well. I just can't always promise that I'll have a man she approves of!

\*

The press is something I've had to try and get used to. I know that without the press I get I wouldn't necessarily have had the success but there are times when it's hard…

Sometimes there are stories that aren't true and they get splashed across all the papers and mags, and I hate that. About three-and-a-half years ago I was papped with footballer Jack Cork. I was in Marbella with a load of mates and we were pictured coming out of a hotel together. We were just walking out with a load of friends behind us and they got a picture. The pictures got sold to the press for so much money. He had a girlfriend, I had a boyfriend and it all kicked off. I was seeing a guy called Joe Hurlock at the time and he was reading all these headlines about me and a footballer, and it was horrible. It caused so much pain.

Joe was a serious boyfriend for me, although we were going through a difficult patch by that point. We met at Harmony Health and Beauty where I used to work. I used to give him massages. Then he started coming in every two weeks and then, like, every four days, and eventually we went out on a date. I did fancy Joe. He looked like Frank Lampard. He was a Frank Lampard double. Our first date was in London. I was already up there with Mum and Auntie Karen so I'd been drinking for a bit when I met up with him. This is pretty gross to admit, but I had drunk so much that I vomited on him and then I passed out. How bad is that? It was so embarrassing but the next day when I had the worst hangover and was back working in the salon he called up and booked in for a massage with me that day.

So there I was feeling rough with Joe booked in at three o'clock. Luckily we had a laugh about it and that was it, we were together for a year and a half. It was very up and down but those pictures with Jack Cork looked like something they weren't and it put pressure on a relationship that was already in trouble. I ended it and he was distraught. I just think I had so much going on that I couldn't cope with a relationship. I wasn't in a good place and I needed that time out. I was right in it at that point. Everyone was wanting me and I was starting up my business, and he had a full-time job as a stockbroker. It got too hard. It all built up, it was all too much pressure. Something had to give in the end and I decided to concentrate on my career. It was a hard decision but it was the right one, I think. He's got a girlfriend now and he's been with her a long time. I saw him not long ago and he's really happy and everything, but at the time he was a mess. It wasn't easy for me either but I had to make a decision. I messed up, probably, but I was young and I wasn't dealing well with all that comes with the life that I now have. It was still quite early days.

Those pictures of me with Jack made me really question everything about what I was doing and the path I was going down. It was the most amount of speculation I'd had about me at that point and people were proper harsh on me. There was one point that I thought: 'What is the point of all of this? Is it worth it?' Social media can be pretty cruel and those pictures seemed to give everyone an excuse to go at me. There was a lot of nastiness. I hadn't done anything wrong but everyone was judging me. People knew that I was seeing Joe and they thought that I was cheating so they called me a cheat and all that. It was hard because all I did was talk to the guy but people were jumping to conclusions.

When you're in this industry, it's so hard sometimes, you know. I'm under the microscope for everything. One minute I'm on a high, like when I went away with the girls (Sam Faiers and Fern McCann) to Marbella when we'd just won the TV BAFTA for *TOWIE*, and then suddenly I'm coming back to a load of negative headlines about me and a footballer. We were all so excited to be on that trip – it was like an Essex bus on that plane – us girls and Mark Wright was on it,* too. We'd won the award and we were buzzing. It was short-lived though, because as soon as that pap was outside that hotel, and got me and Jack, I knew it was all gonna kick off*. I was like: 'Are you joking me?' I felt sick because I knew that when Joe saw those pictures he'd think the worst. I felt proper awful. You can see from my face in the pictures how shocked I was. I knew they would cause a problem straight away and they did. Since becoming famous I've become thicker–skinned and because of that I've learned not to get worked up about what people are saying about me. People judge when they don't know the facts. This game is really fickle; it can be nice one second and awful the next. You sink or you swim in this business and I'm lucky because I've got a good lot of people around me to keep me strong and pick me up.

Sometimes the stories written are just bloody funny, like the one that claimed that I wanted to date Olly Murs. I think someone wrote that I wanted Olly and I to be the next Essex power couple. That sort of thing is funny because it's not true and it doesn't hurt anyone. I can laugh that sort of thing off easily. It's not so easy when people start selling stories on me and I know that Mum and Dad are reading something that's inaccurate about me. I'm really critical about myself in pictures too, but those 'nip shots'* that the paps* get are awful. I can imagine my parents seeing my boobs out in the paper and it's horrible. It's total cringe. Those are the sort of things that I am getting more used to, I suppose. I've learned to try and be positive about everything or I get too down about it. What can I do? It's part of why I am where I am and I have to take the rough with the smooth.

I don't stress out as much as I did, you know. I was always a bit panicky, a bit edgy, like every day. Now I know what the industry is all about. If you let it, it could ruin your life. I'm quite strong. You know me, every day I go out and I get papped all the time. You have to be on it, you can't be looking sh*t; you need to be looking good... that's why when I get a bloke these days I try and have the relationship in private. If they're not in the public eye it can be a lot of pressure and at the beginning when you are just trying to get to know one another it's a pressure I can do without to tell you the truth.

Changing the subject completely – although I have been out with a few dogs – have I told you about my obsession for dogs? I love them. When I was a kid we had Molly the Shih Tzu and Lucky the cat. Lucky was so vicious and I hated her. She would scratch you if you went anywhere near her. Mind you, I was really sad when she died. Mum and Dad got Lucky on their wedding day; she was a wedding present, but she wasn't that Lucky… she was evil! I was desperate for a dog, so I nagged Dad for one and he let us get Molly. Lucky didn't like Molly at all because she was used to having the house to herself.

I'm definitely more of a dog person! I love dogs, I do. Now I've got a baby Bulldog, Leo, named after Leonardo DiCaprio, but I call him Leo. Actually, half the time I call him Arg, you know, after James Argent, because he's got a big collar with a bow tie on it! Ha ha! You know how much I like to dress up, so dressing Leo up is no different.

Leo spends half the week at school being trained! They train him, like in obedience and making sure he's exercised. Bulldogs need that kind of training because they are powerful dogs and they need agility training. He loves it there, I think he loves it more than being at home with me! When Ruby comes to pick him up he goes crazy and when he gets back he's like 'bleurgh'. That dog rules this house and he costs me a bloody fortune. Probably more than childcare! Leo hates being walked. If I want to get him in his bed, all I need to say is 'walkies!' and that's it, he's in his bed. It was my Auntie that told me about Ruby because she met her in Tesco! She told me that she was proper glam and amazing with dogs, and that's when I got in contact with her! We've actually become good mates and Leo loves spending time with her.

I've got a pug, too, but she lives at Mum's and Dad's house. We got her when I was 17 and I lived at home. We still had Molly but I really wanted a pug and Molly was getting old and she was quite sick. Mum let me get a Poochie pug and she then rescued one, Pugsie, and then I got another one with an ex-boyfriend after I'd moved out called Prince Childs. LOL. See what I did there? Prince Childs lives at Mum's now, so that all the pugs can live together and have company. So we've got Poochie, who is now eight, Pugsie, who is five, and Prince Childs, who is four. Prince Childs is my favourite! Leo loves them but they hate him because he's so much bigger and they're scared of him. Leo's a stinky little thing, though. I've got a cleaner in once a week and I mop the floors every day, but if I go out and come back in all I can smell is dog. It's minging. Seriously, it's nasty. But I love him. I took him to the warehouse one day. You should never do that and I learned the hard way. He was only a cute little puppy at the time and I thought it would be nice for him to come in and meet everyone. Everyone's like: 'Oh my god, it's a dog!' and they loved it, until he literally pooed in the middle of the floor. I had to evacuate. It was so awful. There was me in the middle of the warehouse clearing up dog poo. Can you imagine? Everyone had to be evacuated out the building, it was gross. Note to self: how to ruin your business... bring your dog to work. I won't be doing that again in a hurry, I can tell you.

Growing up I never really had any other animals apart from those sea monkey things. You know, those dried bits of nothing that you put in water and then they come alive? Yeah, I had some of them at one point. Could barely see them in the tank. But seriously, what is the point of them? Random.

Anyway, enough about my dogs and family pets I could write a book just on my pooches but I'll stop there...

When I was 16 Mum and Dad sent me to a private beauty college. I didn't want to do anything else and it was something that I really enjoyed. I went to Brentwood Academy in Brentwood.

I was very confident, more confident than the other girls, and I walked in every single day looking immaculate. Even if I knew I was going to have to take my make-up off because we were doing facials that day or something, I still put a full face on before I left the house, and all the girls used to go: 'Amy will be famous'. They were obsessed with how I always made an effort and how immaculate I always was. I never believed them, I was like: 'No, I won't.' At the time I had a gorgeous boyfriend and I think they thought I was trying to be the next Posh and Becks!

It was a nice feeling being top of the class when I got there. A new feeling. But, when it came to getting my diploma, I struggled. I was brilliant at the practical side and got top marks, but the theory part let me down again and I had to have loads of extra lessons to help get me through. I finally passed it after three attempts. Finally, I was a qualified beautician. Despite everything I've done since, nothing compares to that feeling that I had on the day when I found out. A feeling of 'yes, I've only gone and bloody done it.' It was brilliant. That feeling of success is addictive, actually, and I think that was the beginning of me wanting to be successful in everything I did. It didn't need to be big or make loads of money, it was about making sure I was the best, and since then I've always felt like that. You see, I'm a successful businesswoman now in my own right, but I'm not like Karren Brady or Michelle Mone, who are fiercely ambitious. In a way, my success came by small, tiny steps. For me, it wasn't about getting loads of dosh, it was about me as a person being successful in something that I had a passion for. I totally admire women who have always known they want a huge career and then have gone and made that happen. My way has been different, though, and has come out of nowhere. I'm proof that even the girl next door with four GCSEs can turn it around. If the press are to be believed, I'm more surgery-nosed than hard-nosed. FYI, I have not had a nose job, okay? LOL.

While I was on the course I had a Saturday job, so I was getting to practise everything too. I only found this out a couple of years ago but, apparently, Mum asked her mate Wendy to give me the job. Because Dad had all the flowers on his stall, Wendy would buy flowers for her salon, Essence, from him. Mum did a deal with her where she gave me £20 every Saturday and Mum gave her the flowers for free. Mum wanted me to get a job and to start learning about being in a work place, and Wendy didn't really want me on a Saturday. She didn't really need anyone, but I changed her mind straight away! So Mum said to me at the time: 'Oh Wendy's

Me and my mum, Julie, at my christening. The outfit my
mum put me in was beautiful. She looks so happy.

I was three here. Looking very confused in this picture.
I always had very beautiful outfits that Mum bought for me.

OMG, I love this picture. We always used to go on holiday with
Harry and my family. I loved being with him and still do now.
He was such a cute baby. I used to tell everyone he was my
brother because we used to look so alike.

Look at mine and my brother's cheeky faces! Okay, so what was
with our haircuts back then? I remember Billy being really
naughty and always getting told off by Mum and Dad.

Me at my first house in Chadwell Heath. Just look at that armchair! I'm sat
on Harry's Mum (Auntie Karen)'s lap. Everyone used to say I looked like
Karen when I was a toddler, which I think really shows here!

Loved my holidays with my family, I was in Portugal here. I could swim but I always preferred to have my armbands on. Haha, look at my fringe…

We were always away on holiday with my cousins Harry and Ronnie. Auntie Karen would always be taking pictures of us when we were younger. My family would always know how to keep us quiet for five minutes… #icecream.

This is when I moved into my second house in Brentwood. Harry was always around because we loved being together. I can't believe how young we look and, as you can see, we both loved a picture!

OMG, what happened to my eyebrows?! Just adore this picture.
This was when I first went to Raphael Independent School. I was
really nervous about going there but I loved it from Day One.

gonna give you a job.' I was like: 'Oh my god, Oh my god, I'm gonna get a Saturday job with Wendy!' I was SO happy. Wendy had a little salon and I absolutely loved it.

I can remember my first day. She went: 'Right Amy, can you go to Tesco to get me this?' It was a little bottle of bleach, so I went to Tesco and got the bleach. She then asked me to put some down the toilet. I couldn't even open the lid. Mum always did stuff like that. We were never asked to clean or anything like that and she'd never taught me how to open a bottle of bleach, so I hadn't a clue. That sort of thing happened a lot and Wendy was quite a strong character, so I think she was like: 'This girl ain't got a clue!' I think she thought I was quite funny but it was probably annoying too. Customers would want coffee or tea and I'd take the order, get back to the kitchen and have to go back and ask again because I'd already forgotten what they wanted! I'd try so hard to remember the things she told me to do but I'd always forget. Wendy would always ask me to go and get the lunch but I'd never come back with the right food. One time Wendy asked me to pick her up a fish finger sandwich and when I got out into the high street I thought: 'They don't really want a fish finger sandwich, do they? Who eats fish finger sandwiches anyway? Everyone likes a chicken salad sandwich, I'll get her that.' I got back and she wasn't impressed but all the girls couldn't stop laughing. In the end, Wendy got the lunches in not me!

But the important parts I was good at and if I wasn't around for any reason on a Saturday clients would ask where I was. I used to get embarrassed about forgetting everything all of the time but I've learned that in business not everyone is brilliant at everything. We all have strengths and if you can't do something then ask someone for help; there's no embarrassment in doing that. A successful business is one that's got a lot of people who all have different strengths and all bring something to the party. There's no shame in needing help. Can you imagine me doing my accounts? No, neither can I. I'm good with people and I make sure that everyone I employ who is customer-facing is good with people. Capitalise on what you're good at.

Once I was qualified I went on the books and I could do treatments and that, and suddenly I came into my own. Wendy was an amazing, unbelievable therapist. She was brilliant and had loads of clients. I spent hours watching her and learning, and she'd give me advice. She was a brilliant boss.

Of course, at the beginning I was doing loads of the clearing up and sweeping the floor. Wendy would give me a list of everything that needed doing so I couldn't forget! I always took pride in what I did, even if it was wiping the basins and I'd always worry that it wasn't good enough but it was. Mostly 'cos I've got OCD! What was really great about my time at Wendy's was that she was really good about letting me watch and that was something my brain could take in and I did learn from. People think it was *TOWIE* that started me but it wasn't, it was Wendy. She taught me so much and was strict so I learned. She was the best teacher. Okay, so *TOWIE* gave me the platform but without that I know I would have been happy and successful in whatever salon I worked at. I felt sure that one day I would have had my own salon and even without *TOWIE* I believe that would have happened. It wasn't long before I had my own clients at Essence who only asked for me – another big confidence boost.

I also got myself a job at Sugar Hut on the door! It was before Mick [Norcross] bought it, but every Saturday night I'd be on the door doing the wristbands and, like, tick them off the guest list, and then someone else would take them in and show them their table and all that. That was where I met Kirk, Mick's son. He was the first guy I had felt anything for since I split with Billy. Not long after Mick bought the club, Kirk manned the door too, and, seriously, I fell in love with him. When I look at him now I think: 'Oh cringe', but I really fell in love with him. When me and him split up I was distraught all over again. What I've always said about mine and Kirk's relationship is that it was like Ross and Rachel from *Friends*. We had that relationship where we saw each other for a while, we split, then we got back together, and it went on like that. We had this sexual chemistry, me and Kirk. It was like we didn't see each other for six months and then when we did, we'd be like: 'Oh my god'. Get back together then break up all over again, that's how it went.

So I worked at Sugar. I was there for about a year and I got a good wage. I loved it; it was really social and I'm a really sociable person like that. I worked from 8.30am to 5pm at Wendy's and then from, like, 8.30pm 'til midnight at Sugar Hut doing the doors. I always dressed up proper glam on Saturday nights when I was on the door. I put a face on and did my hair and would wear a really nice dress, and I couldn't believe it really because it was something that I was enjoying but I was being paid for. I got paid an hourly rate and sometimes they over paid me!

I love working, that's something that I will say. I'm not work-shy and I don't think the world owes me a living. You'll never hear anyone say that I am lazy. I've never been lazy and I'd rather work seven days a week than not do anything. That's what Mum and Dad taught us: you don't get a free lunch in life, you gotta work for it. I want to get that across to you because I think sometimes it's easy to just think: 'Oh well, she got lucky, I can never do that', and yes, I did get lucky, to a point, but I also worked really hard for it. There's lots of people that have been on *TOWIE* and that are still on the show – not all of them are successful are they? Some of them will have to go back to their normal jobs at some point. Being on the show doesn't instantly make you a success. You can give someone a platform but not everyone will use that platform properly.

It's weird in some ways because, as much as we were made to work and earn money, Mum used to spoil us too. Like, when I was seventeen she bought me a brand new Mini Cooper. People couldn't believe it and neither could I, in a way. Mum and Dad were driving round in old cars and there's me in a new one! I used to have to explain myself a lot but I worked and I appreciated it. More importantly, Mum and Dad were grafting all the hours. They worked long hours on Mother's Day, Valentine's Day and Christmas sorting out all the flowers and doing deliveries. Sometimes on Mother's Day, Mum would have to do 50 deliveries in her car. She didn't care any more than Dad did because that was how they funded the nice things for us. That was their motivation. Everyone needs motivation to do well, something to work hard for, or what's the point? I was pretty much the only one that worked out of my mates but I'd get a hard time over Mum and Dad giving me nice things. They'd say thing like: 'Oh, it's alright for you', but it wasn't like that. I didn't get everything handed to me on a plate. I had Saturday jobs or helped Dad down at the market. I didn't see any of my friends working or doing what I did but they still were jealous of the things that I got given. It wasn't like that anyway and I appreciate what my parents have done for me. I'd be explaining this to my friends and I'd think: 'why am I explaining myself to you?' Mum would get well cross about it and tell me to never explain myself to anyone. There are a lot of jealous people out there. I think my parents gave us things as a kind of encouragement for us and to show us that if you do work hard you can buy nice things. I worked loads of hours and although the money seemed good to me, it wasn't and could never have bought me a car – well, a battered old one maybe.

I looked after everything they gave me and they did the same for my brother – it was always fair. He got a brand new Fiesta. Mum wanted to give me and Billy every-thing, everything that she didn't have. We are her children, you know. She tells us that we are her life, me and Billy.

Honestly, I'm not spoilt at all. I have been taught appreciation and I know what it took for them to give us what they did. Mum was pretty cool. Not many mums would know about fashion and what young girls were into, but she could see me putting in the hours at the beauticians and at Sugar, and I remember for my sixteenth birthday she bought me a pair of Louboutins. Can you imagine? I'd have been saving for months and months to get anything like that and Mum would go without herself to do it for us. She was a bit trendy and she liked all the fashion mags. She's not glam herself, she wears stuff from Sainsbury's, my mum!

Anyway, I'm getting ahead of myself, that's what I'm like – once I start, I can't stop! Back to Wendy... It wasn't long before Wendy had some personal issues and the shop shut, so I found myself out of work. I thought I'd be terrified about trying to get another job but I wasn't when it came to it. Me, being me, I knew that I could get another job and there was no way I was going to just sit at home. I wanted to get straight back out there. I was like: 'I'm gonna find a job', and I did. I saw the advert for a beautician in the local newspaper and I went for it. I was only there for about six months and I wasn't happy there really. I loved the salon, it was just a small salon called Panacea Vitae at Hainault Golf Club and although all the girls there were lovely I didn't really have my own clientele. I wasn't used to being so quiet and I like to be busy. Before I'd always seen work as a social thing too. I got to hang out with a load of mates all day and have fun but we were always with clients and having a laugh. At Panacea

I was self-employed I wasn't getting any money in either so I had to leave. My Auntie Tina (we just call her Auntie but she's a family friend) said to me that Epping Forest Country Club was looking for people plus she was really good friends with the owner of the salon, Sharon. The Country Club has got a big beauticians there and a gym. Auntie Tina told me that Sharon was lovely, so I rang her up. I remember everything Sharon said because I loved her straight away. I said to her: 'Hi Sharon, my name's Amy and I'd like to come in. I'm looking for a full-time job.' And she was like: 'Alright darling, when can you come in?' I went down there ASAP and I remember I had on a little grey skirt, a little pink blouse and pointy shoes, and all the girls were like: 'Oh my god, you're really glamorous', and as I walked in I felt like I'd come home. I loved it. All the girls were nice and Sharon was unbelievable. I became great friends with Sharon and her daughter, Jade, and now Jade is my stylist! Sharon gave me the job that night after I'd done my trades test, which is basically a trial where the salon checks your skills and that you're up to doing the job. She said she'd call me later and she did. She said: 'Oh I'd love you to work here.' And I was like: 'Oh my god!' The salon is called Harmony and has amazing memories for me.

About six months ago I popped in and ended up cleaning for her; she needed some help, so I got stuck in. That's just me. Just because I'm well known doesn't mean that I can't help out, does it? I don't like people that get above their station. Nah, not for me.

I went from one extreme to another and I was so busy at Harmony. It was just unbelievable, and over time I built up a massive clientele there. Sharon was the best person ever. I loved her and I love her still now. Like Wendy, she taught me a lot. If it wasn't for Sharon I wouldn't be the person I am today. She taught me small things that make a massive difference when you're working in a business like mine. Sharon is a very warm person. She'd greet every customer with: 'Hello honey, are you alright?' She'd always ask after people's kids or whatever they had chatted about last time – she made them feel special. She has a great memory, unlike me, but that's something that I've tried to work hard at. I looked at Sharon and thought, 'Sharon's got an unbelievable business', and what I learned from her I have applied to my own businesses and to the staff that I now employ. At the time the idea of having my own business was like a million miles away. Just four years on, and look at me. I owe a lot to her. She's got a good business head on her shoulders. Sharon has two daughters, Jade, who I mentioned, and Charlotte. Jade has become one of my best friends over the years and we are really close now. She was another one who predicted that I'd be famous!

She'd say: 'Amy, when are you gonna meet your footballer?' That's what I'd get all the time. They might have predicted I'd be famous but I don't think any of them deep down imagined it would be in the way that I have been. I think everyone thought I'd get together with a footballer and be a wag or something, but I ain't like that. I don't crave that sort of life. I've had footballers texting me and that, but that's it, nothing more. I prefer to be with people who aren't famous and who aren't bothered by fame – it's hassle being with someone famous and it piles the pressure on. It didn't help that everyone thought I looked like Katie Price. I got that all the time and obviously since I have become famous, the papers and mags have made comparisons about us. I think also, because I was immaculate all the time, my mates just imagined that I craved the glam life to go with my glam look! I didn't really, I just like to look nice. Simple.

My time at Harmony really set me up and has undoubtedly helped me with my own business. I was there for, like, two and a half years, watching and learning and bettering myself, and I was absolutely loving it and had no intention of leaving. Then I got *the* call from *TOWIE*... and that's when my life changed forever and there was no going back.

# CHAPTER 3

# PUTTING AMY CHILDS ON THE MAP

*The Only Way is Essex*. Where do I start? Seriously, where do I start? I owe so much to that show and I'll always be grateful for what it did for me and my family. There I was, working for Jade's mum Sharon, doing my thing and being pretty happy with my lot when I got an opportunity of a lifetime. I was earning about £10,000 a year when I got the call on my mobile from one of the *TOWIE* producers. Kirk Norcross, who was, sort of an ex-boyfriend of mine, had given them my number. He'd spoken to me about being in the show and asked me if I was up for it, which, of course, I was.

However, Mum and Dad were against it. They didn't like it that I was going to pack in my job to do this TV thing and they were like: 'Amy, no.' All they could think was I'd become like Jodie Marsh in *Essex Wives* or something like that! They were worried how I'd be portrayed. They were worried that a lot of the people on the show were from rich backgrounds and I just had a normal one and I wouldn't fit in. It drove them mad, the whole *TOWIE* thing, but they eventually said 'yes' to me doing it. I think they're glad they did now! From the first show it was just phenomenal, although they find all the negative stuff really hard to deal with. They hate people attacking me personally, like when I went to this premiere not long after I'd started *TOWIE* and I was wearing a nice little suit and I had a bun in my hair and the next day the papers were saying stuff like: 'Do we want another Jordan?' You do become immune to it over time but it's hard to read that about someone you love. Mum doesn't really take any notice of it anymore and about all the people that are awful on social media Mum just says to me; 'Try and ignore them. God, if you saw these people away from their computer screens, they'd have nothing to say for themselves.' She says it's bred from jealousy. There was this one time when Mum was walking down the road and she heard this little girl asking her mum if she could come into my shop. She told her mum that she wanted to meet me because I was her role model and her mum went mad, saying: 'She's no role model that Amy Childs, she's not a role model, that's embarrassing to think she's a role model.' This girl was only about ten and my mum was really angry. She doesn't suffer fools gladly or someone crossing one of her kids and I think it was all that she could do not to say something but she managed to bite her tongue!

I think she was angry that I was being judged when they didn't even know me. I think Mum was going to say something to her but when she got back into the shop she was quite upset about it all. People are always going to have their own opinions but it's hard for a mum to hear. At the end of the day I'm not on the street, taking drugs and behaving really badly, am I? I like a glass of wine at night time (who doesn't?) but what am I doing wrong? I've earned a lot of money and I'm putting something back, so for that woman to say I wasn't a role model is a bit harsh, don't you think? Mum hears people all the time in the shop talking about how fake I am and, of course, she wants to punch their lights out, but she has to remain professional. Barely anyone knows that it's my mum anyway and if they did they'd probably be really embarrassed that she heard them talking about me!

At some of the pop-up shops we've done people have started talking to Mum thinking that she works for me and not knowing that she's my mum and saying things like: 'That Amy's a bit fake, a bit of a wannabe', and Mum just stays quiet but I know she's gagging to say something and have a right go! Mum tries to defend me without telling them who she is, but I know she finds it really difficult.

I often worry about what kind of role model I am and, like, with everything, all I can do is my best. Bottom line is that there are always going to be haters, but then I think and worry about whether I'd be happy with me as a role model if I had a daughter. I might not have any girls, but who would I love them to look up to? Would I like them to look up to someone like Amy Childs and I think me being a role model isn't so bad. I work hard, I've done well for myself, I look after my family. I'm not big-headed and arrogant.

Actually, I'm quite a funny and kind person. There's a lot worse people to have as a role model, let's be honest. Some of it is probably a little bit of snobbery around the fact that, you know, I've come from *TOWIE*. Actually, I hope that this book will get rid of a lot of those opinions. I just think about the abuse I got on Twitter when *TOWIE* first started. It was so bad. The first night it aired, me and Sam were up in my bedroom, we couldn't even watch it, we were like: 'OMG, we're on TV', and we were looking at the TV thinking: 'OMG, we can't even watch it'. We just couldn't believe it. We were, like, static. But that night on Twitter everyone went mad, and they were vile about us! I've had to become thick-skinned over time, but I wouldn't be human if some of the stuff people said about me didn't bother me. Throughout *TOWIE* I was very upset at times with some of the remarks I got and I couldn't really stand up for myself because I didn't really know what to say. I thought if I said anything it would probably make it worse! I remember Maria Fowler saying to me that I should get my boobs out; she said that getting your boobs out was like: 'playing for Chelsea' and since she said that to me I've really thought about it long and hard, and do you know what Maria... not getting your boobs out is like playing for England.

I didn't want to go down that glamour girl route and that's how my manager got me *Vogue*. *Vogue* was amazing, I could not believe it when Claire called me to say that they wanted me to be in the mag. Even Claire was shocked, I think! I didn't expect to go on *TOWIE* and get into *Vogue*. It was incredible.

I think I was page eight. It was an article called 'Made in Essex' and they literally got a big jug of water and chucked it over me so I looked like a drowned rat. They put me in thick black eyeliner and I was stood in a field. It was like nothing I'd ever done before. They'd say things like: 'Amy, look over there' and they'd quickly take the shot. I think they got 11 pictures of me. It was just so different. They'd stripped away the glam and it was straight hair, totally fashion. I had a massive blazer, the outfits were, like, eight grand and all that. It was proper mental. I did *Wonderland* magazine too, and I think the cast were well jel of that.

It was quite competitive in that show – everyone wanted screen time. In a way, it still is. I don't know if you saw my Twitter feed recently but Bobby was having a bit of a go saying that I was desperate to be back in the show and all that. Actually, I'm not. I'm busy with what I'm doing and, although I'd never say never, I don't think it would be right for me to go back into *TOWIE*. Maybe a cameo, but that would be it. I've come a long way since being on that show and sometimes you can have too much of a good thing. I have happy memories and I don't want to ruin that. When you make the choice to do something, you have to remember that you can never go back, you have to go forward and if you regret what you did, it will always kind of bite you in the arse. Like, I want to be taken seriously in business, so if I'd got my tits out can you imagine how I'd feel in a business meeting knowing that they'd all seen my boobs? How can someone, a buyer for example, look at you and say, 'Yeah, I like her but

I'm a bit uncomfortable about this because I've seen her get her boobs out.'

The thing is, despite all the problems, getting asked to be on a show like that was like a dream coming true. All of us wanted to be famous or a wag! Seriously though, I hadn't given it much thought after he'd asked me and I never in a million years imagined that it would lead to where I am now. I wasn't even sure they'd call me!

When they did, they explained to me that they'd like to meet me and talk to me about this new show.

I spent ages getting ready and Mum spent a fortune on an outfit. I wanted to look my best, as usual! I wore an outfit from Debra's in Chigwell – it was a pretty little dress. There were about three meetings that I ended up having with them and I didn't really know what to expect or what they were going to ask me, it was really weird. They came to Sharon's salon because they wanted to see me in action! I think part of them was interested to see what I really did day-to-day and to try and understand me a bit more. They walked in and saw me with my face full of make-up looking like I was going out on the town! The lady that came to meet me was like: 'Oh my god!' That was the first time that I met Sarah Dillistone, one of the series producers for the show. I think she was shocked with what I was wearing and how glam I'd gone! It wasn't like an interview, but more of a chat where they were asking me what I liked about Essex and general 'getting to know me' questions. It was strange because it was nothing like I thought it was going to be. They asked me if I knew Mark Wright and I sort of did but not that well at that point. I didn't think the whole thing was going very well. They kept asking me what I could bring to the show and I didn't know what to say. I was like: 'Well, I don't know. I'm a beautician, that's all.' I didn't have any answers for them and I started to feel that I didn't know what I was doing or why they'd even bothered to ask me along. I asked them what the show was actually about, because at that point I still didn't really have a clue, and they explained that it was a show about Essex and it was going to be called *The Only Way is Essex*. They said that because I was a beautician and glamorous they had wanted me on the show to spray tan, but then they said I was quite boring. I didn't have an obvious storyline or something they could get involved in. Apart from how I looked, I wasn't offering anything else like, say, Mark and Lauren Goodger could. It was just the glamour that appealed to them. I honestly think if it wasn't for Sarah I wouldn't have actually made it onto the show. She was the one who pushed to have me. She believed in me to be the person I am today and I'll never forget that. She saw something in me that she thought could work for the show and that's how my journey to fame started. Me, Mark Wright, Sam Faiers, Jessica Wright, Lauren Goodger and Kirk were the originals.

Obviously, because Kirk was my sort-of ex-boyfriend they played on that a bit in the show, and they looked for drama wherever there was some. It wasn't really negative to put that on the TV show, but I was with Joe when I started so it was a bit weird, for him more than me probably. But he got it and knew it was a bit of fun and an opportunity for me. The idea of me being famous was a bit weird and I had no idea any of it would end up how it has. Sarah met my boss Sharon and explained what it was all about and I said to Sharon: 'Sharon, this is just a bit of fun, this show. I'll come back to work.' I genuinely thought that I would. I asked her to give me six weeks off for filming, which she agreed to. So she had clients booked in for after the six weeks of filming when I was back. I was a popular therapist so people were willing to wait but little did any of us know that I wouldn't actually make it back to the salon!

My mum spent, like, about six grand on me for that show. She wanted me to look my best on television and she spent a fortune kitting me out. We'd go down to Debra's and buy dresses, like peplum dresses, and Mum bought me a new coat that was a grand. She'd hire me clothes at over £300 for the *TOWIE* balls and there would be themed nights on *TOWIE*, like an Asian night and an Indian night and all that, and we had to go down the market and buy a sari, which cost a fortune too. Mum loves that sari, she's still got it hanging up in her wardrobe. You've got to realise that the whole thing was major for us.

Mum was paying for me to have spray tans and have my nails and feet done because I needed to look my best. We'd go to La Boutique in Shenfield or we'd go into Soho and look at the dresses. She'd buy me a few little Zara outfits but they were all high-end – no Primark for me darling! Nah, I'm not going to lie, I do like a bit of Primark. I got a mac for a tenner there the other day! So, yeah, Mum spent a heap on me one way or another.

So the first scene of me in *TOWIE* was me in a wedding dress. I don't know why they decided to get us to film there but it was me, Sam and Harry, and I walk out of the dressing room and they're talking to me. I couldn't stop laughing. If you watch it now I look like I'm about to crack up the whole time. It was so weird and I wasn't sure if I was doing the right thing. It was all around Kirk and that was how they sort of introduced my character and they'd set the whole thing off, so when he called me he knew what I was talking about and that. I came out wearing this massive white dress and saying that Kirk had just called me but he wasn't my type. I was like: 'He's a bit of player but I want someone to look after me', and all that stuff. It was totally random but it was really funny. No one knew what to say or talk about! It was in that scene that Harry went 'shut up' and there was no going back! The Essex language was born. Totesville*.

So, obviously *TOWIE* comes out on a Sunday night and we all knew it was going to be on. Not one of us knew that it was going to be such a huge thing but we knew we were going to be on telly. It was a weird feeling, not knowing what to expect. Sam and Billy came over to mine to watch it, and Mum and Dad were there on the sofa waiting to see, finally, what this programme was all about. Then the opening credits come on and Sam and I ran upstairs shrieking. We were up and down like a yo-yo. Every time we were on the telly, we'd put our hands over our eyes and run away from the screen, shouting 'oh my god!'. Literally, I can't watch myself on TV. There we were on TV when actually we are so normal and sitting at home with our parents! Like, can you imagine that? I can't really explain it properly but we just couldn't believe it.

*TOWIE* was a really strange idea but somehow it worked. I didn't know Lauren Goodger, I didn't really know Mark and all of a sudden we were at this sort of party together. So, it was all quite scripted but I don't think that's anything that anyone would be mad about. They chose people who they thought would make good telly and I think we did! I must have done because they kind of made me the star of the show in a way – I was in every scene, you know. There was no lying-in for me because they needed me every day. I'd given up my salary at the salon. I was on £6.50 an hour, although my tips were really good – sometimes I'd make, like, £45 in a day. So, giving up all that was hard because for the first year I didn't get paid at all by *TOWIE*. Nothing. So I relied on Mum and Dad for pretty much everything like new clothes and make-up. I know, crazy! I'm so spoilt but, you know, in *TOWIE* we had to look perfect all the time for filming. We had to have brand-new clothes all the time so that we looked the part! We had to look our best, you know. *TOWIE* wouldn't give us money for clothes or anything and it wasn't until the second series that I got paid £50 a day. It was nothing really and we had to film from six-thirty in the morning until maybe nine or ten at night. Sometimes we'd be filming from seven in the morning to three the following morning. It was proper hard graft and all that. The food weren't great either on set. There was a time when I was a bit like: 'Come on!' But I'm not a diva and I was so thankful to all the runners on the show who did their best to get us stuff. I used to make them all tea because I'm totally obsessed with tea. I drink about 15 cups a day, serious.

What I want to get across about the show is that we didn't know what was happening. We didn't know what we were getting our hopes up for. We were filming this show but none of us knew where it was going. When I was first asked I didn't know I'd be actually on TV, I thought it'd be a bit of fun.

As I said, my mum and dad didn't really want me to do the show at first, they were like: 'You can't go on a show about Essex, because you're gonna be portrayed really bad.' So, I said to my mum: 'Do you know what, Mum? I'm gonna be myself, I'm gonna be my fun self, like I always am, and see how I get on.' Once I'd said that, she told me to go for it. Sarah Dillistone came and met Mum and Dad, and told them what it was all about and sat down with my mum. Even though I was only in two series it became a bit like family. The crew loved my mum and dad, especially my dad because he was making them laugh all the time.

When that first show went out on ITV2 my life changed the very next day. Suddenly my vajazzle course that I did at Brentwood Academy came into its own! Everyone knows what a vajazzle is now. I've become the vajazzle queen! The vajazzle has become mental. Even now in my salon I get about 80 people on a Saturday wanting them done. First it's a wax of their noon* and then I stick the diamantes on! People bloody love it, I'm telling you. It's a phenomenon.

Straight away after that show went out my Twitter went up by 20,000, with people hashtagging '#WhatIsThisShit'. Oh my god, Alan Carr tweeted and everything about vajazzling. It was so weird.

I went down to Tesco the next day thinking, 'I'm Amy the beautician', and I was like a celebrity because everyone was talking and taking pictures of me, wanting selfies with me and all that. I couldn't believe it and when me and Sam went to Lakeside after, people were going: 'Oh my God, that is Amy and Sam!' They knew our names! They were asking for photographs and we were like: 'we're on TV but we're not famous.' But we were because people knew us, whereas before we just walked along and no one looked twice. Everyone wanted a piece of us – it was phenomenal. Magazines, newspapers – they all wanted to know about us.

That's kind of where it all started, because after that nothing ever went back to normal. It was hard, in a way, because it all came overnight. Suddenly I was doing magazine covers with *new!* magazine and then it was *OK!* magazine. I then had an extra pressure and that was how they'd edit me, so each week I'd cringe wondering how I'd come across on the show but as the weeks went by I started to get more and more work. I remember my very first endorsement was at Sally's Beauty Salon. I did a photo shoot for *OK!* magazine there and I had to continually pinch myself to remind me it wasn't all a dream. I'd never earned so much money in such a short space of time. Hundreds became thousands before I knew it. It was mental. I didn't know what I was saying half the time in those interviews. I'd had no press training. In fact, I had no idea what that even was. Ha! I just thought I'd say something and that would be it but that's not how it worked. Once I had management in place, I had press training and I was taught what I could and couldn't say to the mags and newspapers. You know what I'm like – I say it how it is. My filter ain't turned on and I'm far too honest for my own good! Half the time now my manager Claire or Alan (who Claire works with) has to take out things I've said that have come out wrong. Later in the book I'm going to tell you my top ten tips for success and having good people around you is right up there. I can't tell you how important that is.

But back then – when it had all just started for me – I didn't really know what I was doing. I had no management and had all these people asking me to sign up with them and I didn't know which way to turn. It was really hard when that happened. I was just a normal girl. I had no idea who was a good manager or who would do right by me. How was I to know who would help my career or who would rinse me and mug me off? I didn't. Yes, I was making money but I had no proper direction. I didn't know what to say 'yes' or 'no' to, so I did make some bad decisions on the way.

I wasn't short of offers. I had Lorraine Kelly's management (seriously) wanting me on their books. I went to two meetings with one agent but I wasn't really sure it was the right thing to do and then I had people come to my doorstep offering me cheques, saying: 'Amy, I'll give you 50 grand if you sign up with me now.' 50 grand – can you imagine? That's serious money. But deep down I knew it wasn't right for me. I needed a future and to make sure that I did things properly. And that's when I said to my mum: 'Do you know what Mum – I need to get some decent management.' I knew this was my career and that it might only last a year but that I had to make as much money as possible. Instinctively I knew that I needed to be sensible and hatch a plan.

I was a bit of a fan of Katie Price, I really was. When I was growing up I loved Katie Price and Peter Andre, so I'd heard of Katie's manager Claire Powell. All of a sudden I was being branded the next Katie Price and before I got management I was being asked to dress up as her and do shoots, but I'm not and never was like her. It was flattering but it wasn't me and it didn't feel right. I was doing things I didn't really want to be doing and I was going down that road. There's a picture in my house, my mum's got it up. It's a big picture and there's a resemblance there, so I see why people say it sometimes. It was when I was younger and when she was younger that we were quite similar, but not now. I don't think we are anything like each other now. Although I can do a great impression!

After a lot of thinking and not knowing and being unsure about what to do, I met Claire Powell. She had people like Peter Andre and supermodel Rachel Hunter on her books and straight away she seemed like the person that could do a lot for me. I couldn't believe that she would even consider having me on her books, but she did. She saw something in me, like Sarah had. Although, I think when Claire took me on she was actually surprised how big I was. I think she was shocked. Genuine.

Having pictures taken with people when you're out and about is just what happens, I'm used to it now and I'm fine with it. I would never get irritated by that. My mum gets really emotional when I get asked for pictures because she can't believe how far I've come and she's so proud of me. She'll be crying because all these people want to talk to me. She's so proud that I'm a (kind of) role model and that I'm a good person, and that fame hasn't changed me at all. My dad is also very proud but used to be a bit of a nightmare. When I was on *TOWIE* people would walk past his stall down the market and realise it was my dad, and he loved it. So, he started to say to these girls: 'Give me your number and I'll get Amy to call you tonight.' And he made me do it! So I rang this girl up and she said: 'What are you ringing me up for?' She told me that she was at the park and she said: 'see you later' and hung up! I'm serious. It was awful, but that was Dad. He told them I was going to ring so I had to and I did! He'd also try and get them all autographs, so he'd come home and make me sign a load of pieces of paper. He always said that it was important for me to communicate with the fans because they've done so much to help me. It's like the *TOWIE* tours that happen every Saturday… half the time these kids don't see anyone from *TOWIE* when they visit the shops and that, so I always make sure I go down on a Saturday, even now, to sign autographs and chat with people. It's so important to be in touch with the people that are buying your products. I need to hear what they are saying or what they dislike or want more of. That really matters as I try and expand my businesses.

I can remember my first meeting with Claire like it was yesterday. I was a bit scared in a way because it was out of my comfort zone and she said to me: 'What do you want to do? What is your dream?' And there was only one answer: owning my own salon. That was my big thing. Ever since I was 13 years old, I knew I wanted to have my own salon, that was my key thing – to have my very own Amy Childs salon, whether I was a celebrity or not. That was what I had always dreamed of doing. I told her that I'd love to have my own perfume and look at both of those dreams. Claire has always said to me that I'm like a young Joan Collins! She says she has never seen me not looking glam and perfect, and she loves that about me.

Claire said she'd never considered taking on someone from *TOWIE* before me – I mean, she had people like Rachel Hunter on her books – and now she's managed me for, like, five years! She said she thought I was a really nice girl and that I was funny and glam. There was something about me that she liked and thought she could work with! Me and my mum went to meet Claire at her house, also where her office is in West Sussex. Mum was going to me in the car: 'Stop putting too much make-up on, Claire needs to see the real you. Stop putting all that make-up on your face.' I only had a bit of mascara on, for God's sake! It was really nerve-wracking because I'd grown up with Kate and Pete (as in Katie Price and Peter Andre) on my telly so I knew who Claire was and I couldn't believe that she'd even agreed to meet me, but everyone was telling me that she was the perfect fit for me because she is known for making her clients like family and a success. I am so close to my family that it really appealed to me. Now, Claire is, like, another mum to me and that's why we argue now and again – like I would with my mum. I know she is only looking out for me but if I'm not getting it from her in the neck, I'm getting it from my own mum! I get it left, right and centre sometimes. In fact, Mum and Claire are like best friends now. We all laugh about it a lot but in reality I listen to everything Claire says and I really respect her. I always admired what she did with Katie Price. She's a great businesswoman and the fact that she'd even meet up with me was amazing. When Claire first met me I think she thought I had potential, but after *Celebrity Big Brother* it went to a different level, which, when I came out, we capitalised on and it was massive. She knew I was into my beauty and fashion so I could see when we met that she already had ideas of what we could be doing together. I could see her brain ticking!

Claire got to know me pretty quickly and worked out who I was as a person and the fact that I am a family girl. I might seem very strong and I know that on the show I came across as this bubbly, fun-time girl, but I do have a side that is insecure. A side that most people never get to see… and it was there from an early age.

I started to become aware of myself when I was about fourteen – boys began to find me attractive. I never had a boyfriend, though, until I went out with Billy. I had the odd smooch, but that was about it. I was always a bit different like that and all the teachers loved me because I was such a goody two-shoes! My brother was much more confident than me. He was a good-looking lad and he was very outgoing. All the girls used to love Billy and he was definitely much more popular than I was. He had the chat, you know what I mean? I've got better as I've got older, definitely, but he was much louder than me at school. He was a good kid too. Actually my brother got Head Boy at Raphael and then the year after I got Head Girl. I think we were the first brother and sister to get that and Mum loved looking at the plaque on the wall in the hall and seeing our names. I think that made her quite proud. It was good too, because I might not have been the brightest but I had good manners, was polite and the school recognised it which I think sets a really good example. I know that gave me a lot of confidence as a person. Billy was more academic than me and he found education much easier. He'd always try and get the high grades, whereas I didn't even get worked up about stuff like that.

I was never jealous of Billy or anything but he was quite lucky because school wasn't a real trial for him in the way it was for me.

They used to say my brother looked like Charlie from Busted so wherever we went, people would go: 'Oh my god Charlie from Busted is over there!' Billy actually had the same opportunity as me to be in *TOWIE*. Billy could have been really big in the show, but his ex-girlfriend didn't want him to be on it. It's a shame, really, because that relationship never lasted and he could have been on the show. Billy's never been bitter about it, though, or jealous. We ain't a jealous family, we don't have it in us, and Billy would never treat me badly because of what I've done, but I think he'd have been great on the show and I know that he regrets not doing it more than anything. When he split with his girlfriend I helped him buy her out of the house he had bought with her so it was nice to help him. That's a really nice feeling.

Although Billy would have liked to have been on the show, he is successful in his own right now. He works for Dad full-time and he's also a singer. He sings at Sugar Hut, he sings at Suite 104 in Brentwood and other big bars, and he makes good money. Hc's successful, he's got a beautiful house, a baby on the way and he's happy and that's the most important thing. 100%.

Because I was so aware of myself and wanting to look a certain way, I hated the fact that I had small boobs. Who could have guessed that small boobs would have come back into fashion like they have now? I was totally flat, like two fried eggs. I hated them and I knew that the minute I was 18 I wanted to get a boob job. I literally had no boobs – I was, like, a double A, and I had to wear those horrible chicken fillets all the time. There was this one time, I was at Sugar Hut and I had four in to make my boobs look bigger. I was dancing and they fell out on the floor. I was so embarrassed because everyone was screaming and shouting and pointing at them on the floor. It was awful. When I got home I said to my mum: 'That's it. I'm having my boobs done.' Mum knew then that I wouldn't stop until I'd had them done. She thought I was mad and that the whole thing was ludicrous but she knew how much I wanted to have surgery and I think she was scared that I'd go and do it on my own, so she helped me. She found the best surgeon, Dr Carver, and did all the homework and that, and she came with me to the hospital. She didn't want me to have it done, she thought there was nothing wrong with me, but when I want something I am quite determined and strong-minded. Mum's head was pounding when she left me. She was panicking like anything that something might go wrong while I was having the op done. We never told Dad because he'd have gone mad. It took me three days of wandering round in bandages and in a mega amount of pain to finally admit to him that I'd had it done. Mum was really scared about what he was going to say, but he was actually alright. He wasn't impressed but he was like: 'Why Ames? Where's my Amy gone? You are so beautiful, why are you doing this to yourself?' I don't think he was angry, he was just upset that I was messing with myself. He thought I was beautiful, natural and that I didn't need to mess with that.

So I had my first boob job when I was 18. I went from a double AA cup to a D cup. I chose them extra high profile implants so they were not too natural and not too fake. I didn't go for the tear drops because I thought they might drop on me and would be no good for the look I was after. I loved my first boob job, it gave me real confidence. Like, before I'd never have undressed in front of a boy or anything because I thought I looked like a boy myself, so that first boob job did help me feel less self-conscious. I don't regret having them done the first time but I do think I was too young to have made that decision... But I thought I could be the perfect person and I didn't stop there. Surgery can be addictive I think and it wasn't long before I was going too far with it all.

I want to talk about my surgery a bit because it's played an important part in who I am now and has been a huge learning curve. It is the one thing I probably have the most regrets over. I want to talk about it so I can try and inform people thinking about having work done because, believe me, it ain't all it's cracked up to be. I found out the hard way. Even though I am a beautician, my vanity and desire for perfection got in the way of my sensible head. 'Lost in showbusiness', isn't that what the saying is? I was being offered surgery, right, left and centre for free because I was on the show and I didn't say no. Don't get me wrong, I'm not against a bit of botox here and there but you gotta know when to stop and there are times when I haven't and I've paid the price of that. I still am.

It was after I started in *TOWIE* that I got offered a second boob job. I don't know why I decided to go for it because my boobs were fine. They weren't too big and they suited my body. Like an idiot I went under the knife again when I was 21 and they've never been right. My mum was so mad with me because when I want to do something, I won't listen to what other people say. Sometimes I get it in my head and that's it. I started to do my mum's head in because she couldn't understand why I was making these crazy decisions. She was angry because I'm her daughter and I'm doing serious stuff to my body, and it upset her. I started to look different to the person I was. The more work I had done, the older I began to look I think. I sort of lost that young, fresh look. I don't hate the way I look at all but I know my dad always looks at old pictures and makes comments!

I massively regret having that second boob job. I look top heavy and it makes me look bigger than I actually am. Small boobs make you look a lot skinnier. Imagine if they weren't in, how small I'd look. But I can't deal with another operation. I'm too frightened and the scarring will be awful. I think I'm going to have to wait until after I've had kids and then do something about them. Read on and you'll see why I hate them SO much and why I wish I'd never messed about with myself.

With social media I get called all sorts of stuff and most of it doesn't worry me, but when it gets very personal it's not always easy to ignore. Like, if there's a bad picture of me looking a bit bigger, everyone jumps on it. That's the strange part of being in the press, you can't really get away with anything before it's noticed. Like, when I had my lips done and the papers picked up on it. I started to get all sorts of names hurled at me, with people calling me Pete Burns and all that stuff. I think one time someone said I looked like a blow-up doll. And you know what? They were right. I had gone too far and every time I looked in the mirror I barely recognised myself. At first I denied that I'd had lip fillers. I was scared what my mum was gonna say, but before long I had to admit to having had them done. It was another bad decision and my mum, as predicted, went off the scale. Totally mental, she went. I don't think I've ever seen her that mad, that's how upset she was with me. It comes to something when before you're even 24 years old you have to have corrective surgery, and that's what happened to me. It was like self-harm, in a way. I couldn't stop.

I had had my lips done a couple of times but one time a hard lump formed on the right side of my top lip, which made it look like one side of my face was lopsided. It's such a painful procedure having your lips done and that time it was more painful than ever. I got home and my brother's mate was 'round the house and he was like: 'WTH have you done to yourself, Amy? Have you been in a fight or something?' My lips looked bloody awful and they never sorted themselves out.

In the end I had to have the lip fillers taken out because they looked so ridiculous – they were duck lips and, honestly, having them taken out was even more painful than having them put in. I had no other option – I had become really embarrassed about the way they looked and in shoots I'd try and cover them up with make-up, like foundation, and I'd find myself putting my hand over my mouth to stop people from seeing them. People would stare at me and I felt like they were laughing and I knew I needed to get them out. I let *Heat* magazine film the whole thing because I wanted people to see what I'd done to myself and to try and put anyone off doing it. I lay there, with tears in my eyes thinking: 'What have I done to myself?' It was SO painful and once they were out my lips just collapsed. I hated them. I'd been used to looking at big, full lips and suddenly I had nothing. My lips looked thin and horrible. I cried and cried. Not only had I messed up my lips with the surgery but even after reversing the surgery, my lips had disappeared. Everyone, like my old account manager Nadia, told me that I looked a lot better and a lot more natural but I couldn't see anything apart from thin, horrible lips. Everyone was saying that they just looked thin because I'd become used to seeing huge lips, but that wasn't it. My lips collapsed and in the end I had to have lip filler put back in so that I actually had some lips again. That's pretty bad, ain't it, for someone of 23?

That's why Mum hates me messing with my face because she sees me in pain trying to sort it out afterwards. It's like, she hates my second boob job, which I had two years after my first, when I was 21. She thinks they are too big and I didn't need to do it. She's right – they look bad and I wish I'd never gone through with it. A couple of years ago, I woke up in the night with these awful stabbing pains in my left boob and I was rushed to hospital. It was so painful that I thought my boob was about to explode. It was awful, the boob was hot and swollen, and the whole thing was frightening. I think I was about two-cup sizes bigger on my left than I was on my right. It looked totally distorted and minging. It made Mum even angrier because she knew that I should never have done it in the first place and that the pain she could see me in was my own fault. I had no one else to blame. Mum got so angry at me, my dad got angry at me, so in the end it was not a very happy environment.

I found out after they had scanned it that the tissue inside my boob had come away from the implant and a load of fluid had got in there. It was so bloody painful, I can't tell you. At that moment, I thought again: 'What have I done to myself? I'm here because of vanity, nothing else.' Part of me just wanted them out but the other part of me was scared about going under the knife again. It was a wait-and-see thing because if the swelling didn't go down I would have to have had them out completely. Luckily, they did go down and I didn't have to have surgery or the fluid drained off, but my boobs have never looked good again. Basically, they point in different directions! It looks like the implant has sort of slipped – that's the best way to describe it really. They're too big for my size-eight frame and they look proper fake. I'm not happy with how they look at all and I'd love to get them reduced but I'm too scared to have surgery again. Basically, once you go bigger and then want to go smaller again you have to have your nipple removed and stitched back on again. It makes me feel sick to even think about it. Vom. I don't wanna have patchwork boobs. It's pretty scary isn't it? What more of a warning do young girls need than me not to have work done?

It was the worst press because it was so personal about how I looked and questioning what I'd done to myself. Oh my god, it was horrific and horrible. I'm supposed to be a role model but I was looking more like a freak than any kind of role model. I thought I looked good when actually I didn't look good at all. I was being ridiculed by everyone. It's easy to go overboard with surgery, and very quickly. When I started *TOWIE* I had had my lips done but by that point I hadn't gone over the top, so it looked quite natural, I suppose. But then I started to have them injected, like, every three months and the comments about my face were horrific and they really affected me. Things saying I looked like a freak and disgusting. I'd always been confident about how I looked, so it was hard to hear but even I was looking at pictures thinking: 'What have I done to myself?' I'd even be stopped in the street and asked what I'd done to my face – it was really awful. I'd be upset, Mum and Dad would be angry with me and questioning me about what I was doing and it wasn't a happy time for me. I hate arguing with my parents but this was a huge issue for them. In the end, I stopped telling them what I was doing and I started to go behind their backs like a stroppy teenager.

My happy place is at home with my family and this was massively affecting that. I put it all down to the fame. All of a sudden I wanted out. I thought if I left it all behind and went back to Sharon's I could lead a normal life again and everything could go back to the way it was. My manager Claire was angry with me and Nadia, who was looking after me, kept asking me why I was doing what I was doing. Everyone but me was asking the same questions and, as I didn't have the answers, for a long time I kept on doing it. I decided that I didn't want to be under that microscope anymore and that I wanted out. It was never gonna be that easy and, of course, I'm still here so I didn't make that choice in the end.

Overnight, in a way, I'd become this Essex beauty – glamorous Amy – and then suddenly I'd turned into this, like, surgery freak. I knew that if I wanted to be taken seriously again and wanted my businesses to succeed then I needed to change. I knew I needed to go natural again. Suddenly people started to listen to my story. I was on *Daybreak*, I was on *This Morning*, I was in the magazines because people were so interested in what had happened to me. It's an easy path to go down and I was prepared to talk about it and be honest but most of all I was being honest with myself, and that was a breakthrough. It's definitely made me stronger. Yeah, I picked myself up. I was like: 'Okay, you've gotta start looking different. You've got a business, you've got to sort this out.' My business head clicked in and I didn't want to lose everything because of what I was doing to myself.

I didn't wanna be like Alicia Douvall – I didn't want to be going down that road. Naturally, I think that I'm quite pretty and I wanted to get away from the whole surgery thing. It's amazing how quickly bad press makes you wake up and take notice. It was bad, and I mean bad, but you know what?

It made me stronger. It made me the person I am now. The person who can always surprise and the person you never know what to expect from...

I had my teeth done when I was 22 and I actually like the way my teeth look now but it was so painful to have them done at the time and, again, I'm not sure if I rewound the clock I'd do it again. I was always craving perfection – always wanting to look the best and, with the teeth, it was me wanting to get that Hollywood smile. I can remember sitting in the dentist's chair and looking at myself in the mirror. All my teeth had been filed down to a tiny point and I looked like Freddie Krueger. I wanted to cry because there was no going back. My natural teeth that I'd been born with had literally been filed away. I kept thinking: 'Ames, what have you done?' My teeth were so painful that for a year I couldn't eat solid food properly and I had to drink with a straw. I lost one recently towards the back of my mouth but I'm not having it done because I can't stand the pain to get it fixed. You know what? If I was skint in 20 years and my teeth fell out, I'd just have a mouth full of spikes. These are the bits that people don't realise when they make the decision to have work done. People are shocked that I'm only in my twenties. Part of that is because I have achieved so much and I'm still so young, but part of it is what I've done to myself...

Sometimes I worry what message I am sending out when it comes to surgery. It makes me really sad to think that young girls would get surgery because they want to be like me or they think it's okay because I have done it. I know that I need to set an example but because I've been in the public eye for such a long time, and since I was so young, it feels like I've missed out on some of that time where you can make mistakes. Whether it's having my lips done or wearing a bad outfit or wearing too much make-up, it's all there for me to see the next day online. I can't get away with anything! I look at some of the old pictures and I just cringe. Us Essex girls like a bit of bronzer but that bruised look ain't so good, is it?

I remember wearing so much make-up when I was that age. Mum's got some pictures of me when I was younger, where I am wearing no make-up and now, looking back, I think: 'Hang on Ames, why did you wear so much make-up?' 'cos when I look at the natural pictures of me, I look so much better. I didn't have no lip-fillers in. Like, nothing. I literally looked quite plain and simple. Maybe, like, a bit of mascara but that was about it. That didn't last for long because then I went through this whole phase with just, like, heavy make-up. I looked punched in the face, as though I'd been in a fight or something.

There was this picture of me on Facebook and people were saying: 'Ames, what's happened? Ring me. Is everything alright?' They actually thought I'd been in a massive accident, that I'd had a massive punch-up, but it weren't that, it was the make-up! I basically wore too much of the stuff and, OMG, did I love the bronzer. It was like my go-to thing in my make-up bag and I caked it on! The 'bruised look' I call it, and I looked bloody terrible. I got so much agg over that, I tell you. It was the most awful thing ever.

One time, it wasn't my fault that I looked bad. I'd had a treatment and had reacted to the product, which, BTW, is why you should always do a patch test first. Anyway I had this reaction and I looked like the Elephant Man, I really did. People were saying that I'd had some work done but I really hadn't. I had a black eye and everything! But that was bad luck because it could have been anything. But, of course, everyone jumped to conclusions.

Now I look back on myself, I think: 'Eugh'. I'd have ridiculously false eyelashes on all the time. Now I barely use them. I designed my own range of lashes and if I do wear them I'll wear some of my own. I'm quite lucky because my eyelashes are pretty long anyway but I suppose it's one of the phases that I had to go through. Mind you, even through *TOWIE* I looked different to how I am now. My look was much more full-on and in your face. I was just always very glamorous and when we started to film for *TOWIE* I wanted to look amazing all of the time. Now I'm happy to dress down at times and dress-up for the right occasions. That's growing up, right? I now know that less is more. Well, no, not always; I am from Essex remember? That, and the fact that these days life is very different for me. I'm running businesses, I'm paying salaries and I'm in a totally different space. I'm going to name that too-much make-up look my 'punched look' and it's not a look I fancy trying again!

Talking of Essex, it is like a little bubble in a way. There's not many places that you could go 'round the supermarket with a head full of rollers in and no one bat an eyelid, are there? Round here, that's totally norm*. I wear rollers all day and sometimes I sleep in them so I get the curls in my hair – especially if I'm getting ready for a night out. It wasn't uncommon when I was younger and hanging out in Sugar Hut to have rollers in for at least 24 hours. Then, I'd take hours to put my make-up on and have exactly the right outfit. I used to love all the dressing up on a Sunday night when we went to Sugar Hut. It was my favourite night in Essex and that was even before *TOWIE* started. I'd also go to Nu Bar in Loughton, especially on Bank Holiday weekends. They were the best. We all dressed up to the nines for that night. Oh my god, on those Sundays it was like we was at a wedding, honestly; the beautiful outfits people had on. That's what I love about Essex and why I'll never move away from here – it doesn't happen anywhere else, I don't think. Maybe Liverpool is the closest to it, but I live in a bubble. If I go to Marbella you can spot an Essex person a mile off, I can just tell. Probably because I am a typical Essex girl? Definitely. I'm the one who gets dressed up to go to the pub on a Sunday as if I'm going to a huge party.

I was thinking about Essex just the other day, as 'round here everyone settles down so young. I don't know why but it's true, that's what happens. Part of me wants that I suppose, it's what I've grown up around. Even my parents settled down young. Dad was Mum's second boyfriend. Her first boyfriend, Bradley, was a right sort and Dad is still well jel of him! But then she met my dad, the charmer! Dad's such a character and when Mum first met him he was cooking beetroot to sell down the market. After they'd been together a while Mum would be down there too, and people would call her Mrs Beetroot!

I'm a proper Essex girl at heart and I can't imagine ever moving away. Besides, I've got my work here, all my friends are here. I go to London a lot with work, but I never get tempted by moving there. Nah, I'm not a London girl. I love my Essex. I got all my family 'round here and my businesses; everyone's friendly in Essex. I love an Essex boy. I ain't ever gonna move.

Having said all that, I've toned the way I look down a bit now, like, I've toned myself down in a lot of ways. Three years ago I'd go down the King William pub totally dressed up. I'd never go dressed in jeans, whereas now I do. I was totally different then, I'd have to wear a dress, do you know what I mean? It was a pub but everyone dressed up to go to it. Jack Tweed and Mark Wright would be there, way before *TOWIE* got started. It was the place to be. If you were anyone or wanted to be anyone, you would go there. I used to go there a lot and Mum would keep tabs on me. Actually, I still have to text her every hour and a half when I'm out to let her know that I'm okay. She panics about me. But as long as I text her, she is okay. If I'm going out with the girls – I'll text her and say 'Mum I'm here, all the girls are here. We're all fine.' Then I text her when I am on the way back home again.

Anyway, back to the dressing up – I would wear some amazing outfits on those days, it's really only recently that

I've started to not worry about my best dress when I go down there!

These days I like to do that shading instead of a load of bronzer. You know, the thing that Kim Kardashian does. It's pretty cool but it takes a lot of time. I'm well jel of Kim K – she must have a team of people around her doing all that shading. You can literally change your whole facial shape by doing it but it takes forever. It's so much effort but I can do it. I do it a lot when I go for a night out or something but you gotta have time and you can't rush it!

I hope by the end of this book you'll see the journey I've been on – the good, the bad and the downright ugly at times and how I've overcome massive difficulties to get to where I am today. Yes, I've made mistakes but I'm being honest about them and I hope other young girls won't do the same as me. I want to be talked about because I'm a woman who's done well for myself. To be known as a businesswoman (who is learning every day), because I am, and not some fake, ex-*TOWIE* girl who got lucky.

I look back at pictures of when I was, like, 17 and I looked naturally pretty with my blonde hair and innocent look! I would always get loads of attention, so why I thought it was okay to start messing I don't know. I try to make myself look more natural these days. I'll always be glam but no one wants some over made-up girl turn up to do a job and I've learned over the years that less sometimes can be more. I'm not talking about fake tan, because, in my opinion, you can never get enough of the stuff and you don't want to turn up looking like a ghost either. That's not a good look.

When you are in the spotlight everything gets made bigger than it really is. This whole journey, for me, started totally randomly. One minute, I'm working in a salon on very little money being given extra money by my parents because I can't afford anything and the next I've got photographers standing on my doorstep. I'm being paid for something I love. I love getting glammed-up, I love posing, I love doing photo shoots. I'm getting paid for being me (and to have people like me). I had a moment, not long after it all kicked off, when I thought: 'Why do the press like me? Why do they? I'm just a normal girl from Essex.' I'm overwhelmed by what's happened and I often think, why am I the lucky one? I might not be the most academic person or have the best grades, I don't. But what I do realise is that if you work hard, you will get the reward. It's not easy come, easy go. Every day there's a hurdle to get over. One word of advice, though: when you do succeed, never let it go to your head...

I expect you're wondering why I quit *TOWIE* after just two series? It's a long story, but it was one of the hardest decisions I've ever made. It was a massive gamble and I am lucky because it did pay off, but when I said I was off I was really worried that I'd given up everything I'd ever dreamed of. *TOWIE* gave me this massive platform and there I was chucking it away. I think Mum and Dad thought I was mad, along with a load of other people who just didn't get it, but

I did have my reasons. I was being asked to do all sorts of things, like *I'm A Celebrity Get Me Out of Here* (can you imagine me eating those bugs? No way!), and even *Strictly Come Dancing*, which Claire really wanted me to do. Bottom line, the money was too good for *Celebrity Big Brother* (*CBB*) to turn it down and I wanted to do it. I've watched it for years and I was a fan and out of all of the options that was my favourite. I got a major amount of money to do that show. I couldn't believe the amount – that sort of money was like Monopoly money for me. I was going from barely anything a day to a heap of money, it was ridiculous. It was the first *Celebrity Big Brother* that Channel 5 had done and I had to weigh up whether it was the best thing for me, but you've gotta think about the money side as well, because I could have been going back to work at the salon the next year. None of us knew how long *TOWIE* would last. I knew I had to make the most of the moment.

My manager Claire Powell was telling me that I should leave *TOWIE* but it had become my work, my life. My life had become *TOWIE* and I was so worried that if I gave it up I'd never be able to go back, and then after *Big Brother* finished what would I do? I felt like I was turning my back on the thing that had given me my biggest opportunity. It was the hardest thing ever. I couldn't sleep or anything. Claire was right, it was the best thing for me, of course, but, looking back now, it was such a big gamble to take. Such a big gamble. *TOWIE* wouldn't let me do *Big Brother* as well as the show and I had to make the choice. You do a show like that and it's make-or-break time. People were either going to love me or hate me. I knew that and that's why it was such a huge risk.

But that was the huge turning-point financially for me. Yes, I'd earned good money off magazine shoots and all that, but this was life-changing cash and suddenly it felt like I was making it. That was when I bought my first car. I thought: 'Bloody hell, I've got some money and I can buy a car that I really want!' I bought a Range Rover. I sat there when I picked it up and I wanted to just cry. I couldn't believe it. I was sitting in a car that I'd paid cash for at 21 years old. I'd even bought myself the number plate 'WELL JEL'. LOL. It cost me a large amount because I ended up bidding for it against a footballer. Don't tell my dad that because he thinks I paid, like, half of what I did for it! I sat there and thought: 'I'm just lucky.' I had to pinch myself. My life was on the change... BIG time.

*Celebrity Big Brother* was one of the most scary things I have ever done and I lost so much weight that I looked like one of those lollipop girls. I was skinny with a massive head. Don't forget, I have never been away from my mum for such a long time and, when it came to it, I had a proper wobble. *Celebrity Big Brother* is probably one of the most unbelievable things I've done. It wasn't a job, it was something that I can't even explain. I watched *Big Brother* on Channel 4 when I was growing up. You know, with Jade Goody. I loved it and suddenly they want me for *Celebrity Big Brother*. I couldn't believe that I was going into the *CBB* house. I never thought of myself as a celebrity – I still don't – and that was really weird. I was thinking: 'Am I a celebrity?' That's what I was thinking a lot… I was so worried that I'd walk into the house and everyone would go: 'Who is that? Who is this Amy?' That didn't happen and they all knew who I was but it was a shock to me. It was unbelievable. Kerry Katona was in my year… Paddy Doherty… Tara Reid… Sally Bercow… Darryn Lyons… I loved Darryn Lyons. He became a real friend to me.

But before I went in, I was in a complete state. I was worried about everything but most of all I was worried about being away from Mum. I sobbed that night – I really did – and I wanted to pull out of the whole thing. I knew I couldn't very easily, but I wanted to. I felt sick, I was so stressed out by it all. I kept asking myself whether it was the right thing to do.

The day before I went into the house, I had done an endorsement with Joey Essex and he'd asked me if I was going in and I had to say; 'No.' It was all a big secret until the show went live. The *Daily Star* had called it that I'd be on the show and so everyone was asking me. I didn't feel happy not telling the truth but I wasn't allowed to tell anyone about what was about to happen. I said goodbye to everyone at the Mayfair Hotel in London – I'd done *This Morning* beforehand – and I needed to go somewhere to lose the paps and to change. It really hit me that I wasn't going to see my mum for nearly four weeks. Literally, I just broke down. I totally broke down. I was bad, I really I was. Nadia, who was working with me at the time, was the one who actually took me to the hotel near Elstree and I couldn't even talk to her 'cause I was so emotional. As we were driving out of the back entrance of the Mayfair I was thinking: 'Is this the right thing to do?' I knew I was going to miss Mum and Dad so much. I'd just broken up with Joe (Hurlock), so that was hard too, and stressful. He didn't know I was going in, so I was worried about that as well! That night, the night before I entered the *CBB* house, I sat there alone and thought: 'Oh my god, I'm going into *Celebrity Big Brother* and I'm only 21'.

We were all staying at a hotel around the corner from where *Celebrity Big Brother* is filmed. I had to wear a little black outfit so that I wouldn't be recognised and we all had code names so that the press wouldn't know that we were going into the house. Like, if they phone up the hotel to see if we were there, they wouldn't be able to tell them. My code name was Argentina. I was kept away from all the other housemates too, but I knew all the rumours and I knew that Jedward and Kerry Katona were probably going to be in the house too. Of course, it turns out that *Celebrity Big Brother* was brilliant for me and totally the right thing to do, but at the time I had no idea if it would all backfire or not.

I was so scared about walking into the house in front of everyone, but it was fine. I was well surprised at how many people were cheering me! The whole experience was phenomenal and I think it made me grow up a bit. It did me good going into that house. I met some great people and I got to marry Jedward, although I'm not sure which one it was! Jedward got to vajazzle me too. It was random. I got linked to that Lucien – he was the good-looking one in the house – but I didn't fancy him. I spent my *Celebrity Big Brother* life in a bikini and rollers, as I forgot the cameras were on half the time. LOL.

I don't think Claire, my manager, had any idea how mad our lives would become once I'd gone on the show. It was so amazing that my main business – Amy Childs clothing collection – was created after *Celebrity Big Brother*. I'd always wanted to have my own salon, that was my dream, and I'd never even thought about having my own clothing range, but the idea came along because while I was in the *CBB* house the clothes I was wearing started to sell out in the shops. Mum had bought me a few bits to wear in the house and I bought myself a 'Forever Unique' dress to take in with me too. Mum has always been brilliant like that, she has always bought me outfits and been into fashion. Me going into the *CBB* house was an opportunity for Mum to go shopping and buy me a load of clothes! She had packed me this pug jumper, which I wore, and then suddenly people started to go mad for it. They wanted to know where I'd got it from and, in fact, the guy working at the shop rang Mum up when I was in *Celebrity Big Brother* saying: 'We've sold out'. Just because I'd been wearing it! It was from Minnie's boutique – the boutique Sam and Billie set up earlier that year. So they obviously rang Mum up and said 'Oh my god'. I can't describe it, you know… anything I wore, like a little bikini or a cute top, they were sold out straight away.

When I came out of the house I couldn't believe all the calls I was getting saying that the clothes had basically sold out because I was wearing them. It was crazy. That's where the idea to launch my own clothing boutique came from. People were ringing up asking me to endorse things and all that but I was about to start my own label. Honestly, I don't think Claire knew how big I was until I went into *Big Brother*. That's what she said to me. The power I had even I couldn't believe. Claire didn't know I had this level of following, as in how popular I actually was. I didn't really either. There I was worrying about being booed on the way into the house or that people wouldn't even know me, when in actual fact people liked me and wanted to buy the clothes I was wearing. I was capitalising on something that until that point I didn't even know existed. That, I've learned, is what business is all about: taking the opportunity and running with it. More of that serious chat later…

The *CBB* house itself was better than I could ever have expected. I had brilliant people in there. It was an amazingly weird experience. Being locked up for such a long time without being able to speak to anyone on the outside and, for the first time ever, not being able to speak to my mum, it was very strange for me.

I met so many different kinds of people and people I thought I'd never get on with, like Sally Bercow. I hadn't got a clue what she was all about, but in the end I got on really well with her and I'd never have thought that she was someone I'd have become mates with. I barely knew what she did or who she was. I would talk to her about make-up and hair and she liked me. Although, I don't think any of them really understood what I was saying half of the time and they probably just got pissed off with my hair extensions lying around. I had long, red hair and there'd always be one that had fallen out that someone would find! Bobby (Sabel) mugged me off all the time. He was a model but he was warning Lucien off me and all that stuff when Lucien and I were just flirting a bit. Nothing more than that. And Paddy Doherty, he was a right laugh, but he had his moments when he was unbelievable. And, he broke down in the house a lot. Everyone was like: 'What the hell?' When he broke down I felt well uncomfortable. I started to feel nervous because, even if you do know some of the people in the house, you don't really properly know them. I had to share a room with them all! I was in there with David Hasselhoff's ex-wife and Pamela Anderson, who was nuts. She was hilarious. She would be, like, hallucinating or something in her sleep, and come to all of us, like, patting us at night-time. Tara Reid was also crazy. She barely ate a thing and all she drank was coconut water. All I heard was her talking about coconut water. If I didn't hear coconut water like five million times a day then something was wrong! In her American accent she'd be like: 'I need coconut water.' That's what it was like, all the time! The shared-toilet situation – that wasn't good. Not good at all. You couldn't even have a poo without them listening. Nah, it's bad. I used to go in there (the toilet) with my little bottle of fake bake and sit in there for, like, ten minutes. You've got microphones everywhere. There aren't cameras in the toilets, but there are microphones so they can hear what you are doing! That's hard, isn't it? Me being young and all that.

I was very conscious that I looked good all the time. Always. I looked at *Celebrity Big Brother* as a job and I wanted to look my best, so I glammed it up as much as possible. I knew I wasn't in there to just have a good time, it was a way of people getting to know me outside of *TOWIE*. I wanted to try and get people to know the real me. That's one of the main reasons that I did the show. You can become labelled on *TOWIE* quite quickly and I wanted people to see me, the Amy that my family know. On *TOWIE* I was portrayed as quite a loud character but in reality I'm not. In *Celebrity Big Brother* what people saw was me, there was no game plan or anything. When I got out people said I was a lot more quiet than they thought I was going to be. I suppose I seemed more in-your-face in *TOWIE*. I kept myself to myself and I think they thought I was going to be like going on about *TOWIE* and keeping on about Essex and all that and I wasn't like that at all. I was quite flirtatious with Lucien but I'm a flirtatious person. I always have been, but I don't mean anything by it.

I suppose part of me saw *Celebrity Big Brother* as an opportunity to launch myself as a different person – for people to see me differently – but my main thing was to go in there and be me. I'm a fun person and I'm normal, and I think that's what people liked about me. And then, when I got out, I had my own television show on Channel 5, *It's All About*

*Amy*. What I'd wanted to do by being a part of *Celebrity Big Brother*, I had achieved. People liked me, they had seen me not just as Amy Childs-off-of-*TOWIE*. You see, when you try, put in the effort and be yourself dreams really can come true. Even for people like me…

CHAPTER 4

# TIME TO START A NEW CHAPTER

*It's All About Amy* was a documentary, fly-on-the-wall type programme that was supposed to show me embracing celebrity life. I'd left *TOWIE*, done *Celebrity Big Brother* and this was me flying solo. LOL. It was basically a show following me and my family around – so my parents and my brother and Claire were in it. I couldn't believe I'd got my own TV show. Like, everyone just wants their own TV show and I'd only gone and bagged one on Channel 5. It was just mad, I'd just got out of the *CBB* house and the paps were on me constantly. Already my life was different because I didn't have quite the same interest as I did when I got out of that *CBB* house. I loved the idea of the show because my fans could see what was happening. They could see the journey I was going on and what the reality of it all actually was. I had all my pugs in the show too, so it was much more about finding out about me. It did pretty well, as ratings go. Nothing like *TOWIE* but it did well. The thing is, with

*TOWIE* it was all drama. Mine was just no drama. It was just very natural. People loved it but everyone said: 'Amy's show flopped', but it didn't. My show didn't flop, it just didn't get the viewers in the same way as *TOWIE* did and I was always being compared to that. The *TOWIE* lot are strong as a group on TV and to be successful outside of that I think you really have to think carefully about what you do. I know I did. The idea that I could do anything just because I was a hit in *TOWIE* was rubbish. Joey Essex has had quite a bit of success with his own TV shows and that's reem*. He found something a bit different to do and it worked. I think a lot of my power and success simply came from the fact that I was the first to do what I'm doing, a bit like he was.

It wasn't recommissioned and I guess I did feel a bit crap about that, to tell you the truth. I was riding high and that was the first knock, in a way. Of course, I now know that there are lots of knocks in this game and you just have to pick yourself up and brush yourself down, but at the time it hurt. I felt like a bit of a failure and I questioned, again, my decision to leave *TOWIE*. Maybe I was nothing without that show…

I think it's normal to feel like that. I think you always have a doubt in your head. Will this be the last day of the phone calls? Is this my last month or year of doing really well? Next year will I get the amount of work in? I panic all the time about that sort of thing. Even now when I have much less reason to worry! Success, in a weird way, is an addiction, I suppose. My boutique is doing brilliantly, but, of course, I worry whether the sales of the clothes will slow down. I've always got that doubt in my mind, but sometimes it's quite good to have that doubt because I want to fight for it more.

When the show stopped, Claire and I were already working on the clothes business. Claire had really seen an opportunity for me to create something BIG after *Celebrity Big Brother*. For ages we concentrated on creating a successful business. Apart from the odd pap picture of me in the media, I was barely in the press at all. I kind of needed to relaunch myself, rebrand myself. I had loved every minute of everything I had done but I needed to concentrate on something that would be a bit more long-term for me. Claire and me, we had big plans and behind the scenes we started to create something really different and really amazing – Amy's Boutique was born.

The website was the first thing that we launched. We had a massive launch party at Gilgamesh in London and it was amazing. Peter Andre presented the show – which was basically me doing a catwalk showing off all my dresses. We had a huge stage built and a huge 'Amy' logo above it. We wanted to make sure that it was the perfect night to literally launch the beginning of my business life. Loads of celebs turned up, I think there were about 240 people in total, which included press and family and buyers. I was terrified before I walked out on that catwalk. Terrified because I might fall over (LOL) and terrified because I was worried what people would think. I had everything riding on it being a success and I felt sick with nerves. Of course, looking back – I had nothing to worry about and it went amazingly – I was blown away by it all. We had eight other models who learnt routines and quick changes, and I did a chat in front of everyone to explain the business. It was something else, it really was and when that website went live – it went mad. Proper mad. We had eight other models who learnt routines and quick changes, and I did a chat in front of everyone to explain the business.

None of us could have known how well the dresses would do. Of course, we all believed that what we were about to embark on was going to be pretty special and although we were quietly confident, I don't think any of us could have imagined how major it all became overnight. That's why we started off small, with just 12 dresses (they all had different women's names – all my dresses are named after women) to almost test the market. We only had about a month's worth of stock, as in dresses and packaging, and on that weekend that the website went live. We sold all of them! It was mad. The level of interest was incredible, and it was all out of my mum's house! As the days went by her house was gradually taken over by all the stock, literally sparkly dresses hanging everywhere. We had to get a stamp machine and more importantly we were running out of dresses – we almost couldn't keep up with the demand. Somehow Claire managed to call in some favours and get some material from Paris and got it on a flight over so that we could have the dresses made up urgently. It was a huge learning curve for all of us and quickly we realised that there was no sign of it slowing down and that we had to move out of Mum's – if nothing else, so she could get her house back! We rented a studio that was much bigger but very quickly we grew out of that too, and the stock was piling up around our ears. I wanted the business to be in Essex, near me, but we desperately needed bigger premises so we moved everything down to a space near Claire's office. We didn't know how long the whole thing would last, so it wasn't huge, but we did it up and kitted it out so that it looked a lot more professional and we had a proper customer services – there were four people by that point just dealing with customer services. I think we stayed there for about a year until, yet again, we started to outgrow the space. I really wanted to move it all back to Essex and we found a massive warehouse and we moved everything into there. It's huge and so we have the space to set everything out and sort all the packages properly. It's 10,000 square feet, with offices and warehousing, just as we want it. Because it's so massive we also do a lot of the distribution for other companies like Gemma Collins and that helps spread the cost. All these things I have to think about now!

At that point – when the business was really beginning to take off – I think everyone thought that I'd dropped off the face of the earth, but I was working away behind the scenes to create a really successful business. Everyone, pretty much, has had a crack at opening a shop or starting a business of some sort and I didn't want to be the one that failed. I wanted to make a success of myself and as the business went from strength to strength – all the worries that I had when I left *TOWIE* started to fade away. Things got crazier for me almost as soon as I left the show, it was weird. The opposite of what I thought was going to happen actually happened!

Claire and I are in the business 50/50, and we work really closely and well together. I know what I like and what I want, and Claire helps me with the business side. She knows what's a good deal and what isn't. I am learning and I try really hard. Like I said, the website was the first project and once we had the warehouse and everything pretty much licked on that front, me and Claire set up Amy's Boutique, which is also near where I live in Brentwood, Essex. It was life-changing opening that shop, a lot of work but life-changing. I couldn't believe that I had a shop with my name over the top and that people were driving miles to come and see it and buy the dresses. I still drive down the high street and see people holding bags with my name on and it feels weird. I don't think that will ever change.

All of this has been a massive learning curve on so many levels. Right from the beginning when I had to raise the money to go in with Claire. I had made a bit of money on some of the endorsements I had done and the various mag deals while I was in *TOWIE*, and obviously I had the money from *Celebrity Big Brother* by then, so it was a big gamble to put up all the cash I had, but it was one that I wanted to take. I could have gone out and bought a load of stuff, but I didn't, I was sensible. I did have to go without things because I wanted to invest my money. Whenever I meet celebrities a lot of them say to me: 'Always invest your money.' You always hear about celebrities going bankrupt and I don't want to be one of them. I don't want to throw these opportunities away. Because it was the first time I'd ever done anything like that, as in putting up a heap of money, I was quite nervous about the whole thing, but Claire has done it before and she is much more ballsy than me. I'm learning to take more risks and be braver. Claire is the bold one, not me! Claire and I are different but similar in some ways; we bring different things that you need in a partnership.

Once we had the money things started to happen quickly. Suddenly I was involved in all these meetings and I found them hard. I've never been in a meeting with accountants; it's just not me, is it? Just imagine me sitting there with all these people talking about numbers... it's a joke! I'd try so hard to pay attention and to listen, but every couple of minutes my mind would wander off or I'd start looking at my phone. I always carry a nail file on me, so I'd get that out and start filing my nails! I wasn't being disrespectful, I just found those meetings really, really hard. I still do, although I'm learning that the nail file isn't always appropriate! Every time that I'm in one of those kinds of meetings – I try my best to learn something new and to pick up something from it. Gradually I have built up more understanding of business and how it works. I'm never going to be the next Karren Brady, in that I need much more help along the way, but I know I can be successful if I work hard and learn as I go. I think a lot of people are very successful because they have a team of people around them that they can trust and I have that. Everybody plays his or her part. I'm the face of these businesses, but there is a lot of hard work and effort that goes on behind the scenes and I owe a lot to the brilliant people surrounding me.

I went out of the press for quite some time but it wasn't time off... I was still working a lot. I was probably working more than ever, trying to make a future for myself.

It was kind of difficult to leave behind the Amy Childs character because, bottom line, that was me. I didn't act or put on a show and the commitment to leaving behind my youth at 21 years of age was well hard. I didn't want to leave Amy behind, but I did want to get taken seriously in meetings, and when I had some good ideas I didn't want people just to look at me like I was the pretty one in the corner. It was weird because on the one hand I was 21 and on the other I suddenly had to be a businesswoman, a career woman. It didn't really feel like me. I'd gone from doing vajazzles and having a laugh on set to suddenly being involved in buyers' meetings, which I had no clue about, and then, recently, meetings with stores like Lipsy or Next or Dorothy Perkins, but it made me grow up quicker. Yeah, it made me grow up overnight, but it was hard. At the time, I'll openly admit that I liked the fame and that I liked the paps taking pictures of me. That's a love-hate relationship and, as time has gone on, I don't perhaps love it as much as I did at first, but I'm not gonna lie, I liked it. Then, suddenly I had to come away from the press because Claire wanted me to step out of the limelight a bit to concentrate on everything with the business, and I'm glad that I did because it was all so full on that not having the press attention gave me a bit of a breather. It's easy to get carried away and that time away from the chaotic craziness gave me the time to think exactly what I wanted to do and how I was going to be Amy Childs the businesswoman, and how I was going to make my business amazing.

I think my private education helped me quite a bit. I always wanted to be successful as me, but I didn't want to become someone different, I can't emphasis that enough. Like the posh voice – I had it for a while but I ditched it because it wasn't me. I don't speak like that and I don't think you have to to be successful. It was just the growing up so quickly that was hard for me and trying to understand things I would never have even looked at before. I can't really explain how hard that was for me. I had to understand what a business was all about, how to run a business, how to get staff, how to sort rotas and I was thrown into that right from the off. I'm glad it happened that way though, because it's made me the person I am today.

I'd have meetings with Claire and, because I struggle with remembering things, I used to write down little notes. I'd jot down things that I needed to remember and if I didn't understand anything I'd phone up Claire later and ask her to explain. I find it hard, but I do always try my best. You know, I didn't have a clue about nothing like that before. I'm not ambitious in the same way as some successful businesswomen. I'm not and I can't pretend that I am, but if it all ends tomorrow I'll be really happy with what I've achieved. In some ways the whole press game and earning money is addictive, but I've done well. Sometimes I think it would be nice to have the success without the fame… I can't imagine how that would feel.

I was talking to Rylan (Clark) the other day and we always chat about how amazing our lives have become. I wonder if he feels the same way as me with the pressure of the media and all that? But, once you've got it, it's hard to turn your back on it and we both know that's what gave us the platform in the first place, I guess. I'm not being ungrateful, it's just that sometimes living your life under the spotlight and having to think about everything I do and everything I say is tiring. It's hard to live my life that way. Look at me and Brad; we are quite private about our relationship and that's how I'd like it to stay. Once the press start talking about us all of the time, the pressure on the relationship gets more and more. But I own properties now and if it did end, I know that I'm sorted for life now. It's pretty amazing to be able to say that at 25 years old. I can honestly say that I'm happy with my lot. I'm not saying that I've given up now. Oh no, I've not done that, I'm always looking for the next thing to do. That, I've learned, is how business works…

Talking about Rylan – do you remember when he brought Nicole Scherzinger to my salon? That was the most random day EVER. I'd never met her before and suddenly she was in my salon being filmed. Rylan and I are like best mates, which is why he brought Nicole, his mentor on *The X Factor*, to the shop. Rylan rang me when I was in the Chinese with Mum and Harry. He rang me twice and then texted me to say 'ring me ASAP'. He asked me if he could bring Nicole to the salon so that she could have a vajazzle and I was like: 'Oh my god, Nicole is going to be at my salon.' It was unbelievable. I'd grown up with The Pussycat Dolls, listening to their music and all of a sudden she's coming to my salon. I was up all night thinking about it, I was so excited about her coming. I was so thankful to Rylan for bringing her to my salon, it was, honestly, amazing. Nicole said to me that I looked like a doll. I couldn't believe it because she is big time.

What goes on in the press definitely affects my business and it's not always in a good way. I think a lot of the girls when they first come and work for me have their guard up, and that's probably a good thing. They all know not to talk about anything important to people they don't know. When the press want to know things about me, paps will often come in and try and get information, pretending to be normal customers, and the girls always have to be very careful about what they say. The paps will try and question them, and with a little bit of experience you kind of get used to how to deal with it and what to say. But for a lot of the girls that part is tricky and I feel bad when that happens. At the end of the day, they are therapists and don't need all that rubbish. They didn't sign up for all that, it's well muggy. I know Hannah, who is one of my best friends and the salon manager, saw it all (the fame, the media, the paps) for what it is after I had my car crash last year in October 2014. I rolled my motor*, didn't I? My white Range Rover, I wrote it off and it was awful. I got back home after and Hannah came over to see me and she couldn't even get in my driveway because there were so many press and paparazzi outside. Times like that are totally mental. I don't like it when that happens and everything goes totally mad. It's quite scary. It was Hannah's birthday the next day and she wanted me to go out for lunch with her, but I didn't want to face anyone, I was still shaken up and I just wanted to stay at home. Hannah, of course, talked me into it. I was sitting in the back of the car and I was jumping at every slight move because I was so nervous after the crash, and then you've got the paparazzi sitting up the bum of Hannah's car. I was wearing a neck brace and I couldn't move my neck at all, and as we walked into the restaurant all the cameras were in my face taking pictures. Hannah was really mugged off* about it. She hates seeing me go through those kinds of things but it's part and parcel of the life I am in and you have to take the rough with the smooth. The payoff is the lifestyle I have and I get that. It's hard at times but mostly I get on with it.

My brain works overtime all the time. I often think I should be asleep the minute my head hits the pillow but it's in the night that I get to think about things. I have little brainwaves in the middle of the night about what we could be doing but I also wake up in the night worrying that people might not like something. It was particularly bad when we started up the clothing collection. I'd wake up worried about whether people would buy into Amy Childs. They're alright watching Amy Childs but would they buy in to her? Of course, in the day I was more rational but you know what it's like in the middle of the night, your mind goes crazy with stupid thoughts. I was tapping into a new market in a way. The people loving the vajazzle wouldn't necessarily have wanted the dresses I was designing. The vajazzle was selling really well, but it's not the kind of clientele that shop in Dotty Ps. Suddenly it was a completely different thing – a gamble, like I mentioned before. Lots of celebrities are successful when they rebrand themselves, like Katie Price. I admire what she has done over the years with her life; she rebrands herself all the time and it's clever because people never tire of you if you keep refreshing the way you do things or your ideas. She doesn't do anything with her eyes shut – she knows exactly what she is doing all the time. I don't mean to go on about Kate, but I grew up watching her show, and then her's and Peter Andre's show, and I saw how she became a business. It made me think: 'If she can do it, I can do it too'. I don't mean that I wanted to be Kate – I don't want those kinds of comparisons happening again – but what I'm saying is that Kate has been good at doing loads of different things and often being successful with things. She's done books, she's done ranges. You name it, she's done it. Really the biggest comparison between us is that we both want to succeed.

When my show ended, I had people saying that I was too big for my boots and that was really upsetting. I even had Sam Faiers slagging me off in her book, she was saying that all I cared about was my management and not my family and it was lies. I was disappointed with what Sam said, but we are really good friends, we go out all the time and everything is sorted. I'm sure she didn't really mean it but I wish she hadn't said it. I think she would have known that wasn't true when she wrote it. That really affected me. Sam's known me since I was ten, so to go and say that without saying anything to me was muggy. She criticised me for leaving *TOWIE* so early when I was so young. I did leave early and, like I said, it was a huge decision, but I was the first to go and make a proper name for myself. Look at me, I'm proud to say that I have made a success of myself. People have followed and done their own thing, but I was the first and I'm turning over good money every week with my clothing boutique. More than I could ever have hoped to turn over. The formula that we came up with has worked. I have the right people around me. I didn't just rush into getting management; I waited and made the right choices. I've also got a really strong family around me and, no matter what problems I face, they will always be there for me. They love me unconditionally and that gives me even more power to succeed.

After *TOWIE* I think I had become known for being this mad Essex girl. I'd come up with sayings like: 'well jel'. I remember watching the jungle (*I'm A Celebrity Get Me Out Of Here*) and Ant and Dec were saying 'well jel', and I remember looking at the TV thinking: 'I made that word up!' Which I did. All my vocabulary was: 'Oh shut up', 'babe' and 'honey', so it was a bit of a transition to then suddenly get taken seriously in business. I knew what I wanted, and Claire and I knew that we could make it happen but I needed to rebrand myself, but I never wanted to get out of saying those sorts of things because that's me. I talk to people on the phone and go: 'Honey, da da'. That is me. I'm very Essex. I was probably the most Essex person in *TOWIE*, or who has ever been on the show. I'm not embarrassed about that. I look up to people like Victoria Beckham, but look at her back in the day, look at how different she was. If you go too far from the person people fell in love with then I think that's a problem. Victoria did it over time and I also have changed so much. Just look at how I dress now; I'm not always wearing my false eyelashes (although I do still love them!) and all that. I've made small changes and, of course, I've grown up.

I needed to get taken seriously. So yeah, I did rebrand myself. I had to, you know. Well not like I had to but I wanted to be looked at a little bit differently. I wanted my clothes to be sold in high-street stores and I didn't think that me going in being all Essex would wash. I had to learn the right way to behave depending on what I was doing. I'm never going to stop saying 'honey', but I toned it down in some of those meetings, that's all.

What people often don't realise is that I've always had a bit of a business mind about me. They didn't show that in *TOWIE* and they didn't show that in *Celebrity Big Brother*. They're not going to show me talking to an accountant because it's boring TV. I think watching me on *TOWIE* was like people's guilty pleasure. People would say to me that they loved me because I was like the girl next door but it was hard because I needed to move forward. Claire knew that I needed to keep the part of me that everyone fell in love with, but also be able to get taken seriously. There is a certain person who is completely amazed by this Essex phenomenon but we know no different. This is just us and when I got faced with an opportunity that would probably never come around again, like launching my own clothing line, I had to take it and make the changes I needed to. I thought: 'I've got to work my arse off now. I have to be different.'

The power that I had in the *CBB* house was immense. Not me, not Claire, not anyone could believe what happened. I remember saying to Claire: 'This is my opportunity. This is my opportunity now. I've got to bring out my own fashion label.' And that's what we did. We got a designer, and we got a buyer to come in who my mum knew – Dionne, who's a family friend – and we started getting things moving. We started off with 12 dresses and we smashed it. That Christmas we sold in excess of £120k of dresses. It was immense. We didn't get all that money, a lot went on paying people and the outgoings, but it was a great start. And, behind the scenes, we were creating a range and re-investing the money. At first it was pretty basic. Of course, we were still looking at material but we needed to invest in finding out who the 'Amy Childs' customer really was. We needed to gauge the interest from people. Like the research we did showed that a lot of people that buy my dresses like those that go over the knee and that aren't too booby.

So, Dionne bought the dresses; she was the buyer. I didn't even know what a buyer was a few years ago! She'd choose a load and then bring them to me and Claire to see what we thought. Claire is very involved and has a much better idea than me about what shops like. I just go with what I like and what I would wear but, again, I've had to learn that you have to take into account what the retailer wants and needs too. So, the first few dresses we did Dionne had chosen and we tweaked, but then I needed to design my own from scratch. Those originals were my own because I had changed the dresses quite a bit, adding extra lace or lengthening or shortening material, but they had the basic outline for us to work from. I remember looking at one and being like: 'that needs a belt', 'that needs a peplum' and 'the peplum on that one is too thick'. When it comes to fashion I have a very clear idea of what I do and don't like. Both me and Claire have strong opinions and sometimes we agree on things and sometimes we don't, but that's all part of being business partners. I wanted to design dresses from scratch, to put a bit of me into all of the dresses. Even if it was just by making them more sparkly or with a v-neck for a bit of extra cleavage, I still wanted to be a part of the whole process from the very beginning. I knew the dresses were going to sell and that it was worth investing more money in. Very quickly we knew how big it was going to be and I was coming up with new styles which would be available in different colours. It was mad.

Those early days were fun. Some days it would be like playing dress-up; every kid's dream! It was an amazing feeling being able to create something that I loved. I have always been interested in fashion and had a very clear idea of what I like. Because of the interest in my style, I could create dresses that I wanted to wear, but Victoria Beckham was my inspiration. I love the fit of all of her clothes and I wanted to make sure that I took the same care with my range. I wanted to create something that I personally wanted to wear and that would eventually be sold to thousands of women. I knew that if I made it work that it would be the best thing ever for me as a business. I knew I had to make it work and that's, honestly, the most ambitious I have ever been. I believed in the product and what we were doing.

Actually, I was on my way up to London when Victoria Beckham was opening her shop and I saw all these people tweeting about it. I was with Hannah and we were like: 'Shall we go and have a look?' Really we wanted to see Victoria herself but we didn't, we just got to look around the shop. I don't think I could afford much in there! Although I did like her sunglasses!

Sorry, back to my dress collection… So, once the 12 dresses were ready I decided to give them all a girl's name. I still do that but I'm running out of names now! This is a bit of a trip down memory lane for me, but here are all the names of all the dresses I have done since the very beginning:

Abby
Abigail
Aida
Alana
Aleisha

Alexandra

Alexis

Alice

Amanda

Amber

Amelia

Amy

Ana

Andrea

Angel

Angelina

Anna

Annabelle

Annie

Audrey

Ava

Barclay

Becky

Belinda

Bernice

Beth

Betsy

Bianca

Billie

Brandie

Bridget

Brooke

Camilla

Carmen
Carrie
Cassie
Catalina
Cathy
Celeste
Chanel
Charlie
Charlize
Charlotte
Cher
Chloe
Christina
Christy
Claire
Clarice
Clemmie
Colleen
Connie
Crystal
Dahlia
Daisy
Dani
Danielle
Darcie
Debbie
Dee
Deirdre

Delilah
Demi
Diana
Dita
Dolly
Dominique
Eleanor
Eleanor
Elisa
Ella
Ellie
Eloise
Elsa
Emma
Erin
Estelle
Esther
Evangelina
Eve
Evie
Faith
Felicity
Flora
Florence
Fran
Francesca
Gabriella
Gemma

Georgia
Gigi
Gracie
Hailey
Hallie
Hannah
Hattie
Hazel
Heidi
Helen
Holly
Iris
Isabel
Isabella
Isla
Jackie
Jade
Janice
Jasmine
Jayden
Jaynee
Jeanette
Jemima
Jenna
Jessica
Jessie
Jo
Joanne

Jocelyn

Josephine

Josie

Juliana

Julie

Karen

Karla

Katlin

Katy

Kay

Kayleigh

Keira

Kelly

Kim

Kitty

Kylie

Lauren

Leigh

Lexi

Liberty

Linda

Lindsey

Lisette

Lizzy

Lois

Lola

Lorna

Louisa

Louise
Lucia
Lucy
Mabel
Madeleine
Maisie
Mandy
Maria
Marissa
Marlena
Marlena
Mary-Lou
Maxine
Megan
Melanie
Melissa
Mia
Micha
Michelle
Millie
Mimi
Miranda
Molly
Monica
Morgan
Mylie
Nadia
Nancy

Natalie

Nicola

Nicole

Nila

Olivia

Orla

Paige

Paloma

Pandora

Patsy

Paulette

Penelope

Penny

Petra

Petula

Peyton

Phoebe

Pippa

Polly

Priscilla

Rachel

Rebecca

Remy

Rhonda

RIA

Rosie

Roxanne

Rylie

Sadie

Samantha

Sammy

Sapphire

Savannah

Serena

Shelley

Simone

Siobhan

Summer

Sophie

Stella

Suki

Sunshine

Suzanne

Suzy

Tabitha

Talia

Tamara

Tamsin

Tanya

Taylor

Tia

Tiffany

Tilly

Tina

Trudie

Tyla

Una

Ursula

Valentina

Valentine

Verity

Victoria

Vogue

Willow

Yasmin

Yolanda

Zara

And I'm now running out of names for the dresses!

Apart from my website – amychildsofficial.co.uk, fashion label 'Lipsy' were the first retailer to stock my dresses. I've always loved Lipsy and from a young age had a load of their clothes in my wardrobe, so to have them selling my dresses was an amazing feeling.

I still didn't have my salon at this point, that came later – I was investing everything I had into the clothing line. The first day we launched my website it crashed. A friend of ours, Tracey, had helped us to set up the website and we had one phone, my mum's iPhone, and the day it launched I thought I'd get about five orders. Instead we sold out in, like, three days. On the first day 300 orders were placed. We could barely cope with the demand and there were about three of us working on it all. It was a very small thing at first. I did a little photo shoot wearing all the dresses. I think it only took about half a day and that was with me having my make-up done too. It was the Bridget dress that really went down well with people; Sam Faiers wore it and it sold out straight away. It was really fitted but ruched on the belly, so it was slimming. I remember putting it on and thinking: 'This is an Amy Childs dress, I love it.' At first we just did it in red and then we did it in different colours, like nude and black. The Jessica dress did well too, because it was really sparkly. It was wraparound and really low cut and booby! I drive down Brentwood High Street sometimes and I see girls carrying bags from my shop and the buzz that I feel when I see that I just can't explain. I can't ever imagine that feeling going away.

I never in a million years could believe what was happening to me. At that point we were doing everything ourselves because when you start a business it's always a gamble. It might not have worked. I believed in it 100%, but at the end of the day it could have gone horribly wrong and I was learning to take those gambles. I had my own money to lose in it as well as Claire's and I wanted more than anything for it to work. But even in my wildest dreams I could never have imagined it doing what it has done and how well it's still doing three years on.

Because the dresses had sold so well, we weren't really prepared. We just had to sort something out. We had to get bigger and we had to get bigger quick. Tracey had to work for us full-time and we had to get more dresses in, simple.

We then had to get a big unit near Claire's house and employ people to pick and pack, and people to do the customer service bit. It just went mad, we didn't know it was going to be like this. We thought, yeah, a few dresses here and there but nothing like that. So, it wasn't a case of expanding slowly, we had to do it quickly because of the demand and I didn't want people waiting for ages for their order or they wouldn't come back. I'm a perfectionist, always have been, and if I'm going to do something it needs to be done properly. I didn't want unsatisfied people or people being aggy* because they didn't get the dress when they wanted it or we sent it out late so they didn't get it for a night out they were planning to wear it at. That's where I'm good, because I know how important it is to make people happy. The business is still growing now.

My salon came after the clothes and then the Boutique in Essex, which stocks all the dresses, came after the salon. We thought it added to the brand to have a shop, plus I could sell all my other bits in there too, like I do in the salon. The salon was more of a passion for me, I suppose. Something I've always wanted to do. It's hard to make money from a salon and so it wasn't such a good business opportunity financially, but this wasn't about the money for me, this was about me doing something that I wanted to do. A dream I needed to fulfil, and suddenly I had the money to be able to do that, which was amazing.

So I opened 'Amy's Salon' on Brentwood High Street. It's funny because, although it's nice to have money I'm not that financially driven, the salon makes me loads less money than my clothing line but my heart is in the salon. It's been open for four years now. On my TV show *It's All About Amy*, I was filmed trying to find a shop that I could start up in. It was harder than you think because a lot were too small or the wrong location and we looked at loads of different options but finally I found a little spot on the high street. And it had parking out the front. It was perfect. I remember I was in Dubai, with Claire, doing some photo shoots when Mum rang me up to tell me that the lease had been signed and that I could start work on the salon. It was an amazing feeling. I can't tell you how happy I was. Suddenly I had two businesses and people employed by me. How mad is that?

When I got the keys to the salon it was in a right state. The doors were off their hinges and the paint was peeling off the walls. It was a complete mess and we didn't know where to start with it all. There wasn't even any electricity. It was ruined and we had to start from scratch with clearing it all up and decorating it. Suddenly I was choosing paint colours and curtain material and all that. I was getting my hands dirty!

One thing I've learned is that you need to be hands-on in business. I don't just sit back and hope that people do the job – I want to have input and know that things are being done the right way. Even now, when the businesses are doing so well, I'm down there every Saturday to meet people on the *TOWIE* tour and to check that everything is being done properly, and midweek I pop in there too.

Generally, 40% of all those walk-ins on a Saturday are there to see me, so I need to be in the salon as much as possible. Like today, if I had nothing to do, I'd be in there for three hours making sure the standards are exactly as I want them to be. I might not be great with the figures, but I am good with people and everything that Sharon taught me that is why I try and teach my girls. The girls also go on regular training to keep them on their toes and to learn new treatments. What is good is that the salon is now busy with regular and younger customers on a Saturday.

I have to be careful too, because the salon is a proper business and I've worked hard to get that message out there, so when the tours come round it can be hard because it's a lot rowdier and there's lots of excitement. At the end of the day, though, it needs to be a relaxing environment for all the other customers, so it's a bit of a balancing act. For instance, when the phone continually rings and people are asking for me over and over again, it gets difficult because you don't want to be rude but at the same time I've got a salon to run! I do as much as I can to satisfy all the people wanting to meet me. I do all the kids' nails on half term. I book out a day to go into the salon on school holidays and I paint their nails. I like doing that and the kids love it too. See, you can be fun in business and I like to think that I bring the fun factor to it.

Having good staff is SO important. I can't be there all of the time and I need to know that when I'm not the salon is working well. I need to trust the girls and that's why it's so amazing that I've got Hannah. I met Hannah about five years ago through a friend and she's become one of my best friends. I've got three besties. Hannah in the salon – she's a really true great friend of mine. Obviously there's Jade – my best friend; she's my stylist and she's like an agony aunt. You know when you've got a problem, you ring her and go: 'What do you think?' and she'll dish out advice. She's always got time for you. Always. And my other best friend is Chanel. I met Chanel in the hairdressers. She was just sitting there and I started talking to her. I'd known of her through Brentwood and knew she was such a lovely girl. The past three years we've got really close. I've got great friends that really look after me.

Going back to Hannah, she's unbelievable and it's lovely to work with someone who is also your best friend. I trust her 100% and she puts 5 million % into it and it wouldn't work without her. The salon is her baby too, so much so that even though she's engaged she has no wedding plans because she doesn't have the time to organise it! She sees the salon like I do and feels the same way about it, in that she is very protective of it, and she has been there from the beginning helping me to launch it and make it a success. It was a real journey even getting the salon in a fit state to open, it was at the time proper minging. Even two days before opening we had painters still in and a few builders. I never thought we'd get it done in time! At that point we still hadn't even done all the training, like till training, which is pretty important! I had organised all of our training to be done at the salon but there was no room to move, so two days before opening when we HAD to have the training the till man turned up and we didn't have any tills unpacked. They were all in boxes in the salon, so we had to get the boxes, put them in Hannah's car and drive to her mum's and dad's house, and we did the training in their front room! You do what you need to do, don't you?

The night before we opened we were all in the salon until about 2am trying to get it ready for the big opening (the mayor came down to open it). Dad came down with his van and loaded up all the boxes because at one point you couldn't even see any floor space!

The day we opened we weren't ready at all! I can laugh about it now but it wasn't funny on the day. We'd organised for the press to come down and they were all due to turn up late-morning. I had the cameras from my show filming and MTV said they wanted to film it too. I was like: 'Are you having a laugh?' It was crazy – so many people, so much mess and loads of camera crews! I was down the salon with Hannah still clearing boxes out at the crack of dawn and then I left everyone else to stress, so that I could go home and get my hair and make-up done ready for the opening. When we turned up it was fine and I was so proud to be able to say that this was my place, my salon, because that was something I had always wanted. I think that's why I wanted it all to be so perfect – the salon was something that I'd always dreamed of having and because it was becoming a reality I wanted it to be 100% right. I felt like a proper grown up all of a sudden!

I was having to think of things like health and safety and stuff I'd never even known about before. We had meetings with people about wallpaper and it felt like we spent more time in B&Q than anywhere else! I needed to remember everything. But in that moment on opening day, I'd realised a dream and I was on a total high.

Me and Hannah are so close that we go on holiday together and go out together, although she likes to party more than me. She's always trying to get me to get a hot tub put in my garden because she says: 'If you won't go out, Ames, I'm bringing the party to you!' It's true, I'm not a big party girl, but if we do go out it's always a big night down Sheesh or something, and both of us always have to work the next day. We roll in and, because we are such good mates, we laugh our way through the day and our stinking hangovers! Personally my favourite days are the girls' shopping in London days, which I LOVE. I go with Hannah a couple of times a year and we get a cab up to London and we go to Selfridges and Harvey Nics shopping and have a couple of drinks in the bars, and then we go for dinner. By this point we are a little bit drunk and every time we go we forget to get our shopping because we've had too much to drink at Selfridges!

Hannah and I have been to Dubai twice together. The first time I asked Hannah to come with me because I was over there doing a photo shoot and I thought we could have a laugh. It was some company for me too. It's hard for us to both be away at the same time, but for a few days here and there it's okay! So, this time that we went (this will make you laugh and show you what a proper ditz I am), me and Hannah went for ten days. I love Dubai and neither of us could wait to get there. I'd had a spray tan before I went so I didn't look all white on the beach. But when we got into our room I looked outside and it was overcast. I was proper mugged off. It stayed like that every bloody day, so we stayed in the bedroom sleeping and that. At night we'd go out and I'd see all these people with red hooters*. I was thinking: 'This is proper muggy now. How are these people going red and brown when there's no bloody sun?' Seriously, I was getting pissed off. I just couldn't understand it. On the last day I opened the room's balcony doors and it was bright sunshine. It turned out that the hotel room's windows were tinted. Can you believe it? It had been bright sunshine that whole ten days, and there's me and Hannah sitting in our room thinking it was miserable outside and fake-tanning every night. You gotta laugh about it now but it wasn't funny at the time, I can tell you. How stupid am I? I had to come back and go to the salon and get another spray tan, I was so white. Honestly, that's what I'm like.

Anyway, enough of my stupidity… back to the salon. I've known Hannah for five years and she is brilliant and I trust her with everything. We met at a clothes party when I had just finished *TOWIE* and not long before I went into the *CBB* house. She gave me a spray tan at this party we were at; it was all a bit random. You know when you just meet someone and hit it off, that was me and Hannah. Like, we have really good banter and it was just fun the minute we met each other.

After I came out of the *CBB* house, that's when I rang her and asked her to come and work for me. Hannah was working at a health-and-fitness place in Lakeside at the time. It was a spa but she wasn't loving it at all. She wasn't doing the stuff that she enjoys and it was taking the passion out of beauty for her. It was different for me – I was doing something I enjoyed working at Sharon's. Hannah had decided that she was going to do something totally different and she'd gone and got herself a job up in the city in an office. She'd been up there for about four weeks when I rang her and asked her if she'd be interested in running my salon if I opened one in Brentwood. She didn't say yes straight away because she'd only just got this job in the city managing an office in Canary Wharf, and she was on really good money. It was a big decision for her because how did she know that the salon was going to work out? She knew that in beauty you don't always make the best money. It was her dad that told her to go for it because he knew, like me, that she had a passion for beauty and that she'd be happy doing it and that was that… she handed in her notice. We met up and then it was just absolutely manic from day one. We had deadlines on the salon, we had training coming out of our earholes, we were hiring beauticians and it was just crazy, but so exciting!

In a way Hannah is in control of the salon on a day-to-day basis. Although I do have a lot of input and there's nothing she'd do without running it past me, she's a safe pair of hands and she sees things in much the same way as I do.

I have a staff meeting at both the salon and the boutique once a month, and I speak to all the girls to check that everyone is happy and to generally have a catch up, I want everyone to be happy and that's really important to me. If the girls are happy they are much more likely to do their best.

How would I describe myself as a boss? I think I'm fair, although I moan at Hannah for bossing me around all of the time, but I don't think I'm too bad. I leave a lot to Hannah but I'll always step in when I need to. Say, for instance, if she has any issues with staffing or anything to do with the public, I'll be straight in there and I'll help and advise Hannah in what she needs to do. We often play Good Cop, Bad Cop, and I prefer to be the good cop most of the time! I think that if you have a problem with someone then there is a way of saying it. Sharon used to tell me not to do things, but she did it in a way that didn't upset me and I respected her for that. I like to think that I'm the same in that way. So, instead of shouting and going: 'Oh my god, why haven't you swept that floor?', I'd say: 'Girls, do you mind if you just sweep the floor please.' It's completely different, isn't it? You gotta think that this is my business and I can't have unhappy customers. If they are, I need to get to the bottom of why. I think because it's my salon you do get people that are just coming in to complain, unfortunately. But you get people like that in the world and no matter what you do – they'll never be happy. You could give them the best service in the world – best treatment, best customer service, presentation, absolutely everything, ten out of ten – and they will still want to complain about something. But that's just part of running a salon, and you have to become thick-skinned.

I do the odd treatment, but not many now. It's taken longer to build up the salon than it has the clothes. Amy's Boutique, which I set up in 2011, has been so successful and people from anywhere in the country can get my stuff online. The salon doesn't have that option, it relies on local people. It's great to have the *TOWIE* fans in, but I want the salon to be useful for older people too. I don't want people in the local area to think my salon is just a fad or a joke or that you have to be one of 'that *TOWIE* lot' to be able to come in. I think at first they imagined it to be a bit ditsy and not very professional, and that was the hard part – changing their minds about it. I wanted them to know that, actually, we are at the top of our game and if you come to my salon you will get a good service. I am competing with so many different salons in Brentwood and as much as the whole *TOWIE* thing is amazing for us, it can also hold us back because people don't necessarily see us as a proper beauty salon. I've worked really hard to change that, and more and more local people come back time and again now. In the salon we offer spray tans, shellac nails, gellish nails and vajazzles (of course) – they are the most popular thing on a Saturday. I get, like, a hundred girls wanting them done each week! Not all of them have it on their noon, some have them on their arms instead. We take a little towel, wash the area, pat it dry and then stick the gems on. They last about three days. I don't think anyone had ever heard about the vajazzle before *TOWIE*. I had said to Sarah Dillistone that I was trained in doing them and so she suggested we talked about it on the show, so we did and it became a craze and still is all these years on! Funny thing is, I've only ever had one vajazzle in my whole life! I'm too busy doing it for everyone else!

We also offer bigger treatments, like crystal clear, which I have done once a month. It's microdermabrasion, which takes a layer of your skin off so your skin looks nice and clear. It's amazing and so good for exfoliation and your pores. I love it. I have to keep coming up with new things to offer people. If I stick with one thing people get bored. They want new things on the market. Hannah is great at thinking of new ideas. When we started we did the usual sorts of treatments like nails, pedicures, massages, you know, all the basic treatments. Then we had to start growing things, like we added HD brows. Quick fact for ya... It was when I was on an HD lash course that Claire suggested all my packaging and logos should be in the colour purple. I wanted everything to be pink and I was adamant, but Claire had a couple of bits of packaging made up and actually I really liked it, so that's why everything is purple! Purple is my new pink. It's on my clothing labels, tan, lashes, swimwear, uniforms... everything! And there are purple hints throughout my salon and boutique.

We also, most recently, launched 3D Lipo. It's absolutely amazing and it's been really popular already. Your body has fat all over and this treatment breaks all the fat cells down and freezes the fat so that it never comes back again. So, the therapist spreads some of this solution on the problem area and then places a machine over that area and the machine sucks up the fat. It's not painful, it just feels a little bit uncomfortable. It lasts for about half an hour and when the machine comes off your skin feels numb. You can feel as though you've got a bit of a dull ache, but it wears off very quickly. It's the first treatment for fat cells that isn't invasive and doesn't involve any surgery. It gets rid of the fat cells and it kind of tones you up. It's pretty incredible really. I've had the treatment once but I barely get time to have it done and although I like to be glam and like a nice figure, I'm not nearly as body-conscious as you might think and I like my food. If I'm hungry, I eat. I don't worry about juice diets or counting calories. I'm not a big snacker and I like to eat one big meal a day, which keeps me going.

But I won't stand still and by the time you're reading this we should be offering cosmetic, semi-permanent tattooing. So, we will do semi-permanent eyebrows, eyes and lips, basically tattooing make-up on, which has become really popular. I've got my eyebrows done, as you know! Basically, every three to six months I like to launch something new and something that other salons don't have on offer.

As much as I love the salon, as I said, it's not my biggest earner. My clothing line is the big win on that front. Salons are notoriously difficult to make money from. It's hard because you've got to pay the girls' wages as well as a load of other overheads. There's more people to pay on a daily basis. Fortunately the salon is doing well but it's just harder work, in a way. I think that's totally normal and I know that with even more time we will become more and more successful, but it's not been an easy path. As I own the premises, I rent a couple of rooms out and make money that way too. I've realised that you have to look at all the options to make sure businesses are viable and work. Like, if the girls go on holiday or are sick, I often need to get other people in quick or there's been loads of times that I've gone in to help out if that happens or to answer the phone. It's a good thing to have me on the front-of-house reception sometimes, because obviously it's nice for people to see me hands-on and getting involved. Hannah will call me if one of the girls are sick and I'll come in and get straight on with the job because I know what I am doing. Hannah hasn't got to say to me: 'right, you need to do this and answer the phone like that', I just slot in and start work.

I don't ever think I'm too big to do that anymore, it's my business and I want it to work. It's always a good thing to see how things are really running. Besides, I really enjoy doing it.

There are so many salons in Brentwood, we have a lot of competition, I think there's about 15 now (so loads). Chloe (Simms) opened a salon doing hair last year and it's doing really well, but businesses like that don't really affect us because we offer different things. We are more of an established beauty salon doing the specialised treatments, where they're just kind of doing your tans, nails, make-up and hair, so it is two different salons really. It's the other salons that you have to be wary of, and a lot of the other

*TOWIE* cast have opened up places now, which is why I have to be ahead of the game, always offering something new and making sure my staff are brilliant. Some of them are doing really well, but I think you need to put in the graft yourself and not rely on everyone else. If someone comes in and wants a picture with me, I say: 'yes, of course.' Why wouldn't I? Never forget where you came from, that's what I think. I've heard some of the *TOWIE* lot refuse pictures and all that, and I can't believe it. Are they joking? We'd all be nothing without these people. Show some respect and give them a picture and an autograph if that's what they want. It makes me sad to think that some of them won't do that and if they don't do well, what do they expect? Awful, isn't it? Hannah is, like, my photographer when we go out and she gets annoyed sometimes with people trying to get in my grill*. I think if she had her way she'd tell people to do one*. It doesn't bother me in the same way, but I remember this time when we were at Potters and it was really busy. Peter Andre was there so you can imagine it was that kind of crowd. Pete was with us and we had just sat down for our dinner. We both had soup and I had a bread roll literally hanging out of my mouth, all crusty bits around my lips because I'd so much lip-gloss on. Anyway, this lady's come up and said: 'Excuse me can we have a picture please?' I had a mouthful, so I said, with my mouth full: 'Yes, of course can you just give me two minutes to empty my mouth', and this lady was like: 'No, my daughter wants a picture now.' She got a bit lairy*. Hannah was all for telling her where to go but I get myself into a bit of a kerfuffle and I quickly let them take a picture, even though I looked minging. Other people think they know me, like they are my neighbour or something. One day, a while back now, I was out and this woman came up to me and was like: 'Alright, Ames? How's you? Oh, how's Mark? Arg alright?' Hannah asked me afterwards who it was but I didn't have a bloody clue! I'm used to it but Hannah still finds it totally weird. It doesn't matter where I am though, it always happens. Even in Selfridges not so long ago, I was having a cocktail (a Pornstar) and this girl came up to me and asked for a picture. It doesn't matter, I like it. I'd probably need to be more worried if it stopped!

Fortunately we've got our local clients in now and we don't just rely on the *TOWIE* lot each Saturday, or some of the crazy fans. Don't get me wrong, the tours do well for us. There are four tours every Saturday; sometimes there's 25 people on the tour and that does bring in a lot of trade for us. I wish I'd come up with that idea – I don't know why I didn't, I could have made a fortune!

I'd be lying if I said that starting up a business was easy. It was probably even harder for me because I (a) had no idea what I was doing and (b) had to prove that I wasn't just some girl off of *TOWIE* having a go at something because I could.

Locals were definitely unsure of what to make of the salon but when we were still there a year on I think they decided we must be okay and that's when we started to get more locals through the door. So, then people start coming in and trying us out, because we're an actual business not just a passing phase, I suppose. Now we get a lot of regular clients, but it's taken three and a half years. I do deals with the hairdressers next door to encourage people in. It would have been great if we could have done hair in the salon too, but it's in our lease that we can't do that because there's a hairdressers next door! If I could have done hair in the salon from day one it would have just been absolutely brilliant. Hair and beauty in one place is what people really want and it would have made life a lot easier. But we can't, so we work with The Vanilla Room next door and hand out vouchers with percentages off different treatments, and it works well. There's also The Brentwood Kitchen, which is brilliant, that's where all the school mums go to, so we've got flyers and details pinned up in there, which gets a lot of custom in. I'm always trying to think of ways to get people through the door. Salons are notoriously difficult on that front.

As exciting as it was to have my own salon, I found it really hard at first (like everything else). There were parts of the business that I had no idea about and I felt a bit useless. I thought: 'I'm trying to understand this, but I'm a bit too young to understand it. Am I going to be successful?' I remember sitting there worrying about all the numbers and how I was going to get on. It's not all about the brains and the numbers. I know that now, but at the time it was proper daunting all that stuff. What I did have going for me was me – Amy Childs! I suppose without me fronting it all it wouldn't work.

I just had to come to terms with it being a new chapter of my life and leaving that old character behind so that I could launch a future for myself. At such a young age that was hard because most of my mates were out and about having fun. That's what you want to do at that age. In some ways I kind of missed out on those years. I'm not complaining, but rather than going out and getting drunk I was trying hard to focus on my businesses. Nothing comes easily; you have to work at it and that's what I did. I knuckled down and grafted. I needed to break away from everyone thinking that I was this person who just said 'shut up, honey' and all that (although I still do say it!). I needed people to see the real Amy too. I wanted to make everyone around me proud, and it wasn't about making mega-bucks, it was about me having a job, me having my own salon and, guess what, it turned out pretty well didn't it?

We soon had ten people working for us. It doesn't seem like many now because there are over thirty people on a salary now, plus everyone at the salon. That's mad isn't it? It's quite scary really to think that that many people rely on me for a salary. When you first start up a business it is really important to be hands on and get stuck in yourself. Not only does it cut costs but it means that everything is as you want it to be. If you have a vision and you know what you want you need to do it yourself, then you can blame yourself if it goes wrong. As the business has grown we have looked at all the different places that we can source materials from. It has been a real experience for me. We've been out of the country to China to look at factories to make sure the working conditions are up to standard, which is really important to me, and also to look at and feel all the different lace and all that. So, we've done our homework. I won't be going back to China in a hurry, though. I think the only nice thing about that trip was the hotel!

Both me and Claire wanted to look at the fabrics of the dresses so we both went to China. Claire has got some amazing photos of us there. I'd just finished in a relationship, so it wasn't the best thing and I was feeling pretty low, but the trip was booked and the show must go on. I had to pick myself up and try my best. I'd never been to China before and, like I said, I'm not sure I'll be going back. I got there and, I'm telling you, it was like a living hell for me. I tried my best, I really did, but no one could speak any English. We had a lady with us who could speak a little bit of English but not much at all. I felt homesick straight away and I knew I was there for ten days. I remember the first time I needed a wee. There wasn't any toilets where we were and I had to use a pot. You know, squat down over a hole. It was awful.

I have never experienced anything like it. I saw babies with no knickers or nappies on. Because it was a very poor area we were in and they couldn't afford nappies, these little babies were just doing the toilet wherever they were. Literally, just going in the street. Also there were dead cats and dogs everywhere, and you know how much I love animals. It was the vilest thing I've ever seen. I'm not talking about dead lying on the side of the street either. I'm talking about dead animals hung up on the sides of the street. I don't know why they were there, but they were just hung up with their fur on and everything. Maybe they were to eat, I don't know. It's disgusting and I felt sick the whole time. I tried not to look, but it was everywhere. It was a right awful place where we went. Claire was very professional and she just got on with it, we had to and we needed to, and in a way for both of us it was the best trip because we were finding new materials and growing our business. I'm a five-star deluxe queen, me. We were staying in a beautiful hotel, it was lovely and we took loads of pictures, but we were travelling a lot and that's when I got to see all this horrible stuff. I'm naïve like that and it was a total eye-opener.

We were travelling around. It was raining and boiling hot, and we went to the markets that were full of all kinds of materials and zip buttons. It was fascinating to see. I was trying really hard to concentrate on what we were there to do – it was the lace that we were really looking at but I was getting distracted easily by what I was seeing everywhere I went.

To top it all off someone nearly ran Claire over. I'm telling you, the whole trip was like a nightmare. We walked and walked and walked and everyone had blisters on their feet. We were like drowned rats at the end of it because it was just boiling hot. We were soaking it was so humid. The factories we were going to were so, so hot, all of it was steaming hot. It makes me feel hot even talking about it. I kept telling myself that this is where it all happens.

We went into another place that made bags and there were thousands of stands. We eventually picked one that could make my purple Amy Childs bags and we ordered 75,000 that would be with us within five months, arriving on a ship. Then, to have my clothing labels made, we designed new clothing swing tickets to go on the dresses, which we decided should be a purple Amy Childs dress on a hanger. I could feel we were getting more organised and even though this was a tough trip – going out at 7am, having a brief meeting about what we wanted to achieve that day and then not being back 'til 9pm with swollen feet and soaking wet clothes – it was well worth it.

The lace is unbelievable out there. You can't get better lace than in China, it was amazing and, although the UK and Europe do the majority of stuff now which I'm very proud of, I would still like to get the lace from China at times. And, as much as I hated that trip, I did learn a lot by looking at the materials and the fabrics and seeing how it all works.

I think I lost about a stone while I was in China, though. It wasn't like my Chinese takeaway food in Brentwood. It was nothing like that. I hated it and I hardly ate anything. The only good thing was that I found a Pizza Hut, although it was nothing like our one in Essex, but at least it was a Pizza Hut and I was so excited about getting a pizza! We walked about ten miles just to get to that bloody place but when we got there no one understood us because we were in China. Nightmare. You see, I try and be all 'business' but really I'm not great, am I? I just try my best.

I refuse to go back. We walked, like, ten miles every day. Also me and Claire shared a room and I'm going to tell you about this. Claire loves her AC (air con) and I hate it.

Claire loves pitch black when she's sleeping and I like to have a light on. We were in the same room together, so you can imagine what little sleep I got. Nah, to be fair we ended up compromising and we kept the light on and put the AC on in the lounge so Claire could feel the cool air blowing through. As I was still dealing with my break-up, I had it all going on in my head making me ill; I was in a country that I hated and I wasn't getting any sleep. It was proper muggy. It didn't even end that well. On the way home we got a taxi to the airport. People had told us that we must use a licensed taxi because people get kidnapped and they told us that we were ten minutes from the airport. So we jumped into a cab and half an hour later we hadn't arrived. I looked at Claire and I was like: 'They were right babe – they're taking us. I knew this would happen. We're being kidnapped.' Claire was trying to phone people and we were getting ourselves so worked up that it was ridiculous. We were in a cold sweat by the time we did actually get dropped (safely) at the airport! But the hell wasn't over. Our plane had been delayed. Nothing was open – we couldn't even get a drink and I was wandering around the airport not understanding a word of anything. You know, like, if you are in Spain you can try and guess but in China the signs were like two lines and a squiggle through it. I had no hope and I was scared. A bloke came over and tried to help us and said: 'Storm. No flight.' We had to get a coach for two hours to another airport and then get a flight somewhere else before we could get on the plane home. It was a disaster

– our luggage wasn't with us and all the material that we were bringing back was in those bags. I have never been so pleased to get home!

China was one of the biggest things I've ever done and a culture I'd never experienced before. Although I hated my time there, it was good for me to see, I think. China has amazing materials on offer and it was the first time that I'd ever seen such incredible quality. I learned a lot on that trip, even though I hated it! LOL. There's SO much work that we do on each project and China filled in a lot of those knowledge gaps for me. I'll talk you through the process we go through to create a new dress/outfit from beginning to end:

1. I give the designer some ideas of a dress that I think I'd like to see made. Long, short, low-cut, strappy, long-sleeved – whatever it maybe – and the designer will sketch the dress on paper for me.
2. Then I look at the dress and say if I like it or not. I wasn't very good at this at first. I needed to see them in the flesh, but I've gotten better and better at looking at sketches and working out whether I like them or not. Now the designer will talk to me about what she's thinking before she starts sketching so that I can have my input straightaway. For instance, she'll say she's thinking of adding a cap sleeve and I'll ask her to add a peplum, so it makes the process quicker and smoother.

3. Then the designer gets the material samples together, and Claire and I work out what we want and what we think will work.

4. Dionne is our buyer so she will go to, like, a wholesaler to get all the material. Still, at this point Claire and I can change parts of the design, like if we decide we want a scooped neck or different sleeves. We now get some of our own material printed and now buy from all over the world.

5. Then the dresses go to be made at the factory. There's no going back on the design at that point – when it goes to the factory, that is it. It's a bit nerve-wracking in a way because even though I am totally happy with the design, there is always a worry in the back of my head that I could have done more. That's the perfectionist in me! I always have a sample made so that I can try it and so can several other people to make sure that our sizing is accurate.

6. I've also got Tracey, who runs the website, and she is proper amazing. She's in charge of working out how the dresses get seen by the public. So she'll be like: 'There are three new dresses this week that we need to tweet about and get everyone talking about them.' She tells me that I need to wear the clothes so that I get pictured in them. The power of me wearing and being pictured in them is incredible. My mum and dad can never believe what a difference that makes. They call me 'the gold card' because if we are doing

a pop-up shop or the clothes show, when I turn up it goes crazy all of a sudden. They can't believe it!

7. Then you've got Mum and a load of other girls in the warehouse picking and packing the clothes to go out to the people who have ordered them all. Mum checks everything and analyses everything to make sure that there are no faults on them. She works in the warehouse every day. It's a bit of a family affair, in a way, and I like it like that. Like I've explained, I've always been close to my family and not having them involved would be unthinkable. I know I can trust them and I know they are always looking out for what is best for me. 100%.

Recently I've done a dress called the Talia. It was mint green and it was beautiful, so I've been wearing that everywhere. It's been a real top seller – 300 dresses sold out straight away, it's phenomenal. Often people order two dresses in two different sizes because they don't know if they're a 10 or a 12. So we always know that one of the dresses will be returned and we have to have a system in place for that too. We need to be able to give refunds quickly and without any hassle otherwise people won't shop again with us. I have four people on customer service now, to make sure that there are no problems and if there are, again, we can sort it out quickly.

At the moment, we get 95% of our materials for the dresses from the UK and because it's all become so huge now, we have employed a driver to pick up the clothes on a weekly basis. I'm really aware that we can't stand still and we are always checking that our material is the best and that there's nothing better for us out there. You can't stand still. I've learned that if you don't change and make things better, you get left behind and others will over take you. I think partly that's why the business has been such a massive success because we produce great clothes that are great quality and if that changed so would the business.

As far as money goes and putting the money up at the beginning, it was obviously a big thing and I had to raise the funds to even get started. It was a make-or-break situation – there's no doubt about that. If this hadn't have worked, I'd have been totally skint, but I wanted to gamble. I wanted to go out there and do it, and I had to carry that big decision. I had to make it work. Up until this point I'd been in the press loads but after *It's All About Amy* had finished I wasn't in the press all the time. It felt a bit weird in a way not to have all that interest all the time. It was nice because I could lead a normal life, but it was weird because I'd almost got used to the paps outside my house and the press writing stuff every day about me. Yeah, there was the odd story, but that was it. It gave me the time to properly focus on what I was trying to do without any real distractions. But I missed it, in a way. It was something I'd become used to and suddenly it wasn't there as much. It was yet another learning curve; another time in my life where I had to grow up really fast. I'd gone from being a girl in *TOWIE* to a businesswoman pretty quickly. I don't know how to explain it, but when I started *TOWIE* I was totally naïve. I was innocent but in such a short space of time I'd had to grow up and learn so much. If I had left it another year this opportunity wouldn't have been there for me. I wasn't in a reality show anymore, this was my real life and that's why I stayed out of the limelight most of the time. It was a choice. While everyone was wondering what I was doing and thinking I'd gone very quiet, I was building and growing my businesses. I think you do have to make sacrifices sometimes and being out of the press was a hard choice for me because I enjoyed it. I didn't come out of the press completely but I wasn't in it constantly like I used to be. I did the cover of a few mags which tied in well with my launches and, of course, I love being glam in the mags but I chose not to do them every week. I'm jumping ahead now but I was very lucky, and surprised actually, because when I did start to do press things again, the interest in me came back almost straightaway.

Anyway I was making money, good money. Money that I just couldn't believe. The dress collection was flying. I needed to do something with all the cash. Yes, I bought some nice Louboutins ('course I did) but I needed to be sensible. This was my future. It was thanks to Mum and Dad, who helped me invest the money, that I started to buy houses.

I bought a house in Kelvedon Hatch. That was the first house I lived in. It was a posh, little estate with mostly bungalows on it, but mine was a tiny house, which I now rent out. Then I bought a house just around the corner which

I also rent out now because I'm now living in a bungalow just a few doors down from Mum. She likes it that way so she can pop in at any time and I like it, too, because I'm not too far away. I loved it when I first moved out, but I was vulnerable, as Mum had wrapped me up in cotton wool my whole life. I didn't really know how to do anything because she had done it all for me!

Mum finds it well tough that I've moved out, and she'd tried for ages to stop me leaving, but in her heart she knew it was the best thing. I've got my own independence now and I love it, although Mum still does a lot for me. She works all the hours helping me with the collection. Mum is so hands-on and is always down the shop or picking and packing the clothes ready to send out to the customers. She does so much for me, with my business and with my home life. She's like Wonder Woman and she never gets tired, she just keeps on going. My house, my mortgage, my electricity bills – she's all over it. I'm trying to understand everything but some things are a bit hard. I don't know what I'd do without my mum. I'd probably be sat with the electricity cut off and no heating! I have learned to use the dishwasher now and I can do the washing, and I can even change my own bed. I'm not lying when I say I had never done that before I moved out.

Because she's so busy with all my businesses and she is so busy with the clothes, she doesn't do much hairdressing now. I think she enjoys it. Even though I'm 25 now, Mum still likes to look after me! She sorts my bills out in the house and makes sure my water doesn't get cut off! I'm living in a gorge little bungalow and I've done it up proper Essex style. It wasn't liveable when I bought it. A tramp would not live in it. It was vile. So I designed the whole new bungalow myself with the architect guy. I'm really proud of myself about that because it's turned out well nice. I won't be in there much longer, though, because I'm goint to buy a bigger house, again down the road from Mum. It's a good area to invest in property, as you've got the train station up the road and they're putting a rail link in here to France, which is why it's getting more and more expensive to buy. In the future I'll get my money back in spades I reckon.

I'm going to rent my current house out. I love it and I don't want any old person living here, so I'm going to rent it to some family. I want to go bigger and Mum wants to go smaller! I feel very safe in my bungalow, I'm bolted in and I've got the dog and the electric gates. I get the odd person beeping their horn as they go past my house shouting 'slag', but I'm fine. It doesn't worry me. Mum doesn't like the idea of being in the house on her own and she wouldn't want to move to a bigger house like I do. I'm not scared like Mum – she worries about people knocking at the door at night and all that. I do get a few people but Brad is here and I don't open the door unless I know who it is. Mind you, the door rings so much sometimes that I think I should just put a sign on the door saying: 'Amy Childs lives here!'

Seriously, though, the reason I want a big house as my next house is because I see it as my family home hopefully! I want to stay there a while and get a pool put in and all that. If I do move again I'll keep renting the houses out so that I can get an income. Everyone tells me that houses are the best thing to invest in, so that is what I am doing. I'm slowly building up my future so that when I do have kids I can give them everything my parents gave me.

I'm very proud of what I've achieved. Did you know that Dolly Diamonds (mine and Claire's company) put the money up for Millie Mackintosh's collection? No, thought not! There are a few surprising things about me. I don't want to brag about it but I'm really proud that I was in a position to do something like that. We thought it would be a really good business opportunity for me and I put in four hundred grand. A lot, isn't it? Everyone was saying to me: 'It'll be massive, it'll be a huge hit, it'll be amazing', and I really thought that she would be massive and that it would be a huge hit with Millie as the face of this collection. We put in 80% of the cash and she put up 20% of the money, so she had a stake. To everyone else it was Millie's collection and I was the silent partner. It was another business venture for me and it seems like a great opportunity. After several meetings we got the range into Asos – Millie was the first celebrity that Asos took on which was incredible. We also got the range into Lipsy, Shop Direct and the House of Fraser. We worked so hard to make it a success. It's quite funny, really, because she would never have anything to do with me, even though it was my money that had got her the clothing range. All I do is play the game and I'm a nice person. I don't pretend to be anything I'm not. You can see by how well my collection is doing. I don't try and get the collection into *Vogue* and I'm not so misguided that I think only *Vogue* readers want my clothes. I know that I need to do all the press and I'm happy to do that. I work hard at making sure there is some brand awareness with people, so I'm at the Clothes Show every year – meeting people, chatting to fans and selling all my products. It's real people that buy our dresses, our real market is the real people and you can't get too big for your boots, you know. As soon as you lose sight of your market, you've had it, it's game over. I think it's really important to go and be on your stand and show your face at these things and meet people. It's important to love the products too, and I love my dresses. Like the Talia dress – I want to wear it all of the time because I like it so much. But I've worn it only two or three times, I think, because otherwise the press would slate me!

That day at the Clothes Show is really hard work. I can remember the first one that we ever did at Earls Court – it was a total nightmare. Actually it was a disaster! We pretty much had no idea what we were doing and it was mad. We had ordered the stock for the stand, to arrive at Earls Court. It was supposed to be delivered first thing but at 9am the dresses still hadn't turned up. There we were, with a stand, pictures of me wearing the dresses but no actual dresses to sell! The show was opening at 10am and we had literally nothing to show anyone. We were in total panic. It all finally showed up at 9.50am and we had ten minutes to get all the stock in, unpacked and on hangers ready for people to see. All the dresses were in individual plastic bags and it wasn't easy to do quickly. We weren't allowed to bring in the crates with the clothes in because it was so close to the public arriving and it could have been dangerous so there was me, Claire and everyone else chucking the clothes onto wheelie bins and dragging them into the show so that we could get it all out. We were dripping in sweat and knackered by the time the doors opened. I don't think any of us even spoke to one another we were so busy and at the end of the night, when it was all over, we sat down like zombies thinking: 'What the hell was all that about?' We had sold everything! Now we are much more experienced at it, we know that we need about 300 or 400 dresses on the stand and we are much more organised! The shows look amazing now. I have the set painted two or three days before the show in my salon/branding colours and that takes time to dry. Then we put up the images of me in the dresses and the branding ready for the goods to get delivered. With the dresses, my sleep rollers, lashes and perfumes and we even have dressing rooms – it looks incred. Much more professional these days! LOL.

I think other celebrities go to the show but just rock up on the big day, do an hour of signings and then get back in their car and get driven home. That ain't me. Even now I get there really early, hours before everyone else, at the crack of dawn and set up the stand, so it's just how I want it. Then, once the show is open, I'm there for the day, except for when I go and sit down and have a bit of lunch, which rarely happens because we are so busy. It's proper graft but it's worth it. It's great to meet all the fans and spend time with them. I won't ever forget that without them I'd be nothing, and I owe it to them to be at the front of that stand, speaking to them and having photos taken with them. Then, at the end of the day, me and Hannah pack up the remaining stuff and I drive the van back home, down the A13 full of all the clothing.

You see, I don't mind getting my hands dirty; I think that's the best way to be. I know I'm very lucky with the support network that I have around me and that's unusual in this industry, because I think a lot of people sometimes would maybe get jealous, but not my family, they just want to see me do well. A lot of the other celebrities that I see at shows see me packing boxes and ask me why I'm doing it. They are off getting a drink or going for something to eat, but I ain't like that. I work my arse off. Ask anyone and they will tell you what a grafter I am. From sitting down and looking at why a dress sold well to making sure that the dresses are perfect seasonally (short sleeves/long sleeves or short dresses/long dresses) and I liaise with our PR and marketing people so we all know what to push on a weekly basis. I have to be hands on and on it or it won't work honey.

Millie Mackintosh is very different to me in lots of ways, and she also had a stand at the Clothes Show, but she wouldn't want anything to do with me when we were there. There was this one time that someone had bought something off my stand and then went over to Millie's and asked for a picture with her. She said 'yes' but she asked the girl to put the 'Amy Childs' bag down. Can you imagine? Seriously, that happened! Thing is, these girls don't want to advertise anyone else's gear, but I don't mind. I don't worry about things like that. Even at the launch of her new range she said I couldn't go and basically barred me from attending, as I didn't align myself with her brand. That's probably another way of saying that she thinks I'm too tacky. The thing is, I wasn't bothered about going anyway, I just thought I might be able to help a bit – whether it was dressing mannequins or getting cups of tea. I don't mind mucking in and I thought I might be helpful. I'm not too proud to help out. As it was, my mum went down (as no one knows her I'm guessing Millie was okay with that) and helped to get the launch ready. It's all weird to me – I don't get that kind of behaviour really. There's no need to be like that at all. She wasn't ever very nice to me and I just don't get it. I've never done anything to her. I'm not trashing her and I don't want this to turn into something where she then gets on Twitter and starts slating me. I just think it's interesting how people are and also because I'm proud that I was able to help fund her collection.

Because my collection was doing so well, I created Key Fashion, which Ashley Roberts was originally the face of. Then Amy Willerton became the face of it. It became really big. It was mainly eveningwear and we just sold a lot of it in various shops and boutiques, through Shop

Direct and through my website. Key came about because I was being asked about creating more eveningwear but it just didn't work for the Amy Childs Collection in that the evening dresses were a different price point to the rest of the collections I have. I don't ever mind trying new things with the collection, but these evening dresses were going over the £120 mark. The best way to overcome that was to have a different collection altogether and one that offered something that was a bit different. I started to sell limited edition dresses from anywhere between £100 to £600 and it provided something to a slightly different market. I always look to do new things and recently we have started to do separates – like a top and a skirt and not just dresses because we think that will go down really well with the customers and in fact it already is. I've learned that it's all about knowing your customer. What they like, what they want to spend and if you get that wrong then the business will suffer. People might not like me, they don't have to like me, but they like my dresses and that is key.

Of course, sometimes things don't work and that's just what happens, that's normal from time to time. We can sit in a meeting for hours discussing a design and think we have come up with the best product ever but when it arrives we might not like it. We all make mistakes and you can't be scared of making mistakes. Very often it's just an adjustment to the sleeves or something but eveningwear just wasn't for the Amy Childs Collection and that's when we thought about opening another company and bought Key Fashion. We then came up with a load of evening gowns, totally different to what my other collection had in it. I like sparkly, so there were a lot of sequins involved!

It's very important to me to make sure that all my fans are happy and that I'm producing clothes that they like and that they want to wear. Sometimes it's trial-and-error; you can't always get it right and I've learned that you have to expect some things not to do as well as others. That's just how it goes. Like the dresses Dita and Fran – they just didn't go down as well with the customers. There wasn't necessarily an obvious reason for why, but they just didn't sell as crazily as other dresses. At first I took it personally, but now I see that it is what it is. Very quickly in business you learn to pick yourself up and brush yourself down. The hits come but you don't fall down for long or else you'd stay there! You gotta fight. Recently we tried putting up our price point a bit and almost instantly things stopped selling. Straightaway we realised that there's a price that people are happy to pay and we had gone over that, so we put it back and now all the dresses are at a sensible price point of roughly £50/£75 a dress. I think we tried selling one of the dresses at £100 but people didn't expect that sort of price, like it just didn't work for us. You know £55 is about right and it's perfect for an Amy Childs dress, I think.

I try to make all my dresses nice and fitted, and a bit different to other high-street dresses, so they have that tailored feel to them. I want them to have a slimming effect but to suit a range of different body-shapes. Of course, there are times when I get it completely wrong. Last year we went totally off of our thing and we were going a little bit more fashion. Fashion doesn't work for me; it needs to be chic and have a nod to the current fashion but it needs to be quite traditional. You need to know your market really well and a person who buys Amy Childs dresses, I've worked out, is someone who's glam and likes a fitted, more traditional dress. The dresses should appeal to the older market too, not just teenagers.

I do other clothes, like onesies for young kids (17–25 year olds). I do a whole load of different ones because I love a onesie myself. I live in them! It's all about doing new things and appealing to different people all the time while keeping your current buyers happy. My ranges are affordable but it's not cheap cheap.

*TOWIE* was the starting point for most of us and for those of us lucky enough to be so successful, we owe a lot to it. Gemma Collins is a friend of mine and I got her onto the show originally. The producers were doing a casting and they asked me if I had anyone that might be good on the show, and I immediately thought of Gemma. That's why she came into series two and, yeah, they loved her from day one.

I thought she'd be an amazing character and I saw massive potential in her because she's a typical Essex girl. Gem is with Claire now too, and has her own range, which is going well, and I know that she has to work really hard as well to make it work.

I know that I'm going on about how hard I find all this, but I think it's really important that people see how I've managed to overcome all the odds to be a success. I'd never have imagined being where I am today, but I am, and I think it's proof that anyone can do it.

This business thing has been a huge journey for me and one that I'm learning from every step of the way. I know my limitations and I know when I'm out of my depth, but I'm not scared or too proud to ask for help. You're not a failure if you ask for help sometimes. I might be able to design the best dress ever, but ask me about my accounts and I'll glaze over, start filing my nails or tell you to 'shut up!' You can't be good at everything. Some people could be, but I ain't one of them!

One thing I am good at, though, is public speaking on things I'm passionate about, as I mentioned before. I might have been a plodder at school but I was confident enough to stand up and talk about something like beauty that I love.

So now my latest venture is the Amy Childs Academy and it's going to be mega. The Amy Childs Academy was set up because I wanted to train people the way that I was trained, so that they are totally prepared for the world of work and can walk straight into a job. It's giving something back in a way. I have my own fake tan, which I created – you know how much I like a tan! Ava, one of my beauty therapists from the salon, does the training workshops. It's amazing that I've actually got my own fake tan for sale. It took ages to create because I really wanted to produce something that didn't have a horrible smell, like most of them do. I had an original tan that went into Tesco, but that didn't do very well so I went back to the drawing board and spent time creating something so much better.

Honestly, the new tan is unbelievable. I am the queen of tan, just so you know, and it's taken me two years to do this formula. Every day I was coming home trying to do a different tan and it didn't work. It was so frustrating but it had to be right. My tan doesn't smell, it hasn't got that biscuit smell and it's got 10% DHA, which means it's not overly dark and it's not really that natural, but it's in the middle and it's worked on every single client that I have had in the salon. It doesn't go streaky and it doesn't go green. Every client that comes in for a spray tan, I always ask them to moisturise all their dry areas like knees and elbows; you need to cake it on to be sure that it won't streak. Although it took a long time to create, it was worth it because now I've got the tan and it's been doing so well we decided to make more of it.

And that's where the Amy Childs Academy comes in… People like Nicky Clarke and Lee Stafford already do similar things to my academy and they're really popular. It's a way of giving your knowledge to other people and training them up to my standard right away. If I ever need staff, I'd look to the people who have been on this course. I think because I've been successful they can learn from that and believe that they can go out there and do the same as me. That's what I want to achieve. I think it's an amazing opportunity for wannabe beauticians.

At the moment I just offer a tanning workshop and it's popular. The colleges buy the tan in from me, but I hope to soon have lots of different beauty courses. I think there is a gap in the market for girls to learn how to do these things properly.

The first time that I went and did one of these talks to a load of students I was petrified. It's quite enormous to do something like that and it was actually quite amazing. I am a perfectionist and to be able to get people to listen to me and train them the way I have been taught is incredible. I'm well jel that these guys get this opportunity because I didn't get it!

I've even designed my very own Amy Childs Academy uniform. The idea behind it was that you don't have to lose your style while you are working. I wanted the girls looking glamorous, but at the same time being practical. We saw a gap in the market, so designed these uniforms for other professional beauty therapists. They come in all different colours. All my girls at the salon wear them and they've been really popular.

Like with the Amy Childs Collection, I have to be very hands on with the salon too. I don't just expect the girls to do everything; I get trained up as well, so that I know what I'm talking about. Even now, four years in, I still go on any new training course and I'd never launch something new in the salon and not have a clue about it. I'll always try and get involved, like with the 3D Lipo training. Me and Hannah went up to train together and we ended up having a really good few days away! Even when I'm away, though, I'm on my emails checking everything is okay. I've told you, I'm a perfectionist!

I'm in the salon a lot making sure the standards are high and that it's as clean as it should be and that the customers are happy. I don't often do treatments these days, simply because I don't have the time, but I do miss it. I like doing the HD brows, spray tans and all that, but it's not often possible. If I am down the salon, I'll often answer the phones while the other beauticians are busy, and after about 3pm – when the schools are out – we get LOADS of prank calls! LOL. It's just kids being silly, screaming down the phone 'I want a vajazzle!' and we get some ruder stuff too, like builders will ring up and say things about what I can do to them. You know, happy endings and things like that. It's pretty bad sometimes but I've got to be professional and kind of half-joke it off because otherwise it would get me down.

I have gone from 'that girl in *TOWIE*' to a businesswoman pretty quickly. Hard work, but I did it. I suppose it was the confidence from the people around me that helped to give me the belief that it was the right thing to do because it was scary. I didn't cut my TV career off totally but I wasn't on TV twice a week anymore, so my profile wasn't up there. I do think that if I'd left it any longer that I wouldn't have had this level of success. I was the first to gamble it all and do this, and then other people that have followed haven't necessarily done as well. I used the platform that I was given properly, I think, and I'm proud of that.

Mum reckons that people become addicted to buying my dresses, in that they like the fit and they come back over and over. They like my style and the way the dresses fit, so once they've had one they always come back for another because they know what they are getting. It's quality but at a reasonable price. They also see me wearing the dresses too. I don't think you can create a range and then not like it enough to wear yourself, I really don't. I love all the dresses that I have created and I've worn every single one.

Lots of other girls have tried to do what I do and, with them being on telly still, I thought they might steal a lot of my business but that hasn't happened. It's pretty powerful stuff when you think about it.

I go up and down the country with the brand and I think, as a team, we really work hard to keep the brand alive. When Mum packs the clothes to be sent out, she includes a little leaflet offering 15% off your first order at Amy Childs. It's got a nice picture of me on it and it gets people to pop in the shop. Often the boutique, which is just down the road from the salon, has a lot of tourists in. They'll always buy stuff but they might not be back for six months, so I need some more regular clientele. The girls working in the boutique let customers know that I have a website because that's not something everybody knows. They think I have my boutique and that's it. When Mum's down at the shop she must say it a hundred times and when we go to the Clothes Show, me and

Claire say it a thousand times – we are like parrots! That's how it has to be – you have to self-promote and with Twitter and Facebook I can do that easily.

I also do pop-up shops, again, to raise awareness of the brand. We rent shop space for a weekend and take a load of dresses with us. We let people know that we have the website and then they can buy online, instead of thinking they have got to come to Essex to buy dresses! We only go for a weekend but it's full on. I meet everyone and do selfies and all that stuff and I often drive the van wherever we are going myself. I always make sure that I go – people want to meet me and see me and I am the face of the brand, so it's important that I'm passionate about it and put in the hours. Hard graft, remember, gets you a long way. When I'm there people will turn up and buy stuff, that's how it works. If you get lazy then why would you expect a business to work? I'd expect to fail if I couldn't be arsed. As well as our website, we managed to get my collection in Lipsy and Next. They wanted to stock the range almost from the very beginning but we wanted to wait until we knew exactly who our market was. At first I did a few signings for people, at the stores, who had been in and bought a dress and even now I love to meet the people who buy my gear. In a way it's a kind of research for me. Then Dorothy Perkins wanted to stock my dresses, which was incredible. I think the deal was that they'd give me six days to sell the stock and it sold out in 48 hours, so it was a massive hit. I still have my dresses stocked in Dorothy Perkins and also Shop Direct and of course on my website.

I keep talking about other women who have been successful and I do think that I am quite different to them. I wasn't born desperate to conquer the world, but my success comes from both luck and hard-graft. I believe that girls can relate to me, they want to be glam like me, and that this has been my USP (unique selling point) in a way. I know you're supposed to be really hard if you are in business, but that ain't me. I can't imagine being hard on people or treading on people to get to the top. No way. I think you can be nice to people and do well. Be nice to people on the way up because when you're on the way back down you'll need them! It's not in my nature to be harsh with anyone. Yes, I have standards and at the salon I do want everything to be brilliant but I'm not going to go 'round shouting the odds at everyone because I don't think you get the best from people by doing that. I'm not on some kind of power trip, I am me, Amy Childs, and I like to treat people the way I like to be treated. You need to have some kind of respect. That's what my parents taught me.

I'm totally prepared for the fact that this can't go on forever. As soon as it comes to an end, at least I can go: 'I did my best and I did more than I ever expected to.' There will be a day when it goes quiet, because nothing lasts forever. When I settle down and start to have a family, I'll look at new things that I can do. I'll always continue to try to do my best. There's always a new challenge, it could be that I move into maternity wear if and when the time comes for me to start a family. There are endless opportunities and, now I know more about business, I feel confident that I can do anything if I put my mind to it. That's something that I never thought I'd say. You ask Mum and she'll tell you that when I was younger that I wasn't confident and I have always had to put in the effort and try. I've never believed in myself fully until now, and even now I don't take that for granted. I'm quite a humble person in a way. I've always had work ethic and I do believe that if you work hard, you will get the reward for it.

## CHAPTER 5

# BACK TO REALITY

It was a bit of a shock to the system, but after a long stint out of the media spotlight I decided to venture back into the world of reality TV! I started to do a bit more press, and both me and Claire decided that after such a long time out of it all it would be good to get back on TV again. The collection was still doing well but it felt like the right time to do something when I was offered *The Jump* on Channel 4. I liked the idea of doing it because it was a new show and Davina McCall was the presenter, so I thought it would be really good. Also it appealed to me because it was a bit different. I wasn't very good at skiing. Actually, I've never skied before, so I was the one out there with all the gear and no idea! I wanted to make sure I looked good, but I was terrified! People were telling me that it was really dangerous and that got me worried. I was also going to be away from my family for five weeks, which bothered me a lot too. It was a big decision for me to make and, I'm not gonna lie, I was scared, but I also thought it would be a good opportunity.

Then I had the time of my life – the best time! – and I loved every minute of being there. Yet again it was another experience for me, even though I was totally useless at it. But you'll know that because I wimped out and I never actually did the jump, did I?!

I was the first female celebrity to be booted off the show and it was so embarrassing, but I just couldn't do it. No way. I was petrified. The coach was trying to get me to stay focused and do it but I was crying; I just didn't want to do it. Because I didn't do the jump, Sinitta got through. Sinitta became a really good friend, actually.

I made some really good friends on *The Jump* and I bought everyone on the show a onesie! I'm so glad I took part in that show because I made some proper friends over there. Sinitta and Tara were the closest to me and they were so much fun to be around.

I was so upset when Tara left because she was hilarious. Even though she used to chat about yachts and supercars while I spoke about the Sugar Hut, we had amazing chemistry and just clicked!

I remember one of the first conversations I had with Sinitta was when all the cast were sat around a table ready for dinner and I said: 'There's a lot of vererity in here'. Sinitta corrected me and said it's 'variety' before laughing. Every time I see or speak to Sinitta, she always says 'there's a lot of vererity in here'. She's so much fun! She introduced me to Simon Cowell soon after *The Jump*. We were at Jason's (Sinitta's boyfriend and agent) birthday party and Simon was there.

Cutting the ribbon at the opening of the Basildon store. It was a crazy experience with lots of press, but the public were amazing.

The opening day of my second Amy Childs boutique in Basildon.

A photo shoot for Comic Relief.

This was one of the
campaign pictures that I
did when I was the face
of Lonsdale.

A night out in London with some friends in 2011.
The drinks didn't stop flowing!

This was a day off in Dubai while I was shooting my
calendar out there. I love Dubai, it's a great place to holiday!

With Claire, my manager and friend, at her son Nysna's birthday party.

Peter Andre and I are good friends. This was taken at Claire's house.

Such an exciting day…
this was the opening of
my beauty salon in Brentwood.

In one of our treatment rooms
in the salon in Brentwood.

This was taken at a friend's party,
I am with my cousin Harry, a friend
Mandy and my manager Claire.

Me checking the cuts and material in one of our factories.

Me checking how some material fits on a mannequin to see if it would work well.

Me and my family together. Family is everything to me and we had such a lovely night at my 21st birthday party.

This T-shirt was a
massive seller for us
when we started the
clothing collection. All
my family love pugs.

I went over and said 'Si, I would love to be a judge on *BGT*, babe.' I think he was quite shocked that I went over so casually but I've always been pretty confident like that (maybe that's the recent businesswoman in me). Anyway he gave me the eye and said: 'I'll think about it darling.' I'm still waiting for that call from Simon but I bump into him all the time at awards and shows, and he always comes up to me, gives me a kiss and a cheeky wink. I'm defs in there with the Cowell. LOL.

I often feel like I am well old before my years and that I've lost myself a bit and I hoped that by going back into reality and being back in the press, I might be the old Amy again. I know that sounds weird but that's how I started when I was 19 years old and the last few years have just become a massive blur in a way.

I've tried my hand at so many different things since *Celebrity Big Brother*. Do you remember the fitness DVD that I did? Sorry, I'm jumping back here, but it was a moment that it really hit me that I'd come such a long way. Oh my god, it was totally mad. I'd been used to going to all different countries like Dubai for shoots and all that. But this trip was different. I was flown to LA and we had it all planned. I changed on the plane into a Zara dress that Kate Middleton had worn and as I stepped off the plane wearing it I was pictured. I made the front page of the *Daily Mail* in that dress and it was incredible. The press were talking about me cracking America. It was an amazing feeling. When I got to the hotel after being pictured by all the waiting paps, I couldn't understand how this was all happening when a year ago I was at Sharon's salon. I looked around and there's all the camera crew there to shoot me for my own DVD. MY OWN DVD! It was proper mental. As always, I just did as I was told. They were going: 'Right Amy, I want you to do this and that. Stand here, stand there. Jump up, jump down.' It's a very strange feeling when something like that happens because it suddenly dawns on you that everyone is there because of me. You can see how people get carried away with that because it's a big ego trip. I just felt lucky and so happy for it to be happening. That time was the biggest blur of all because after *Celebrity Big Brother* I was massively in demand, doing all different shows and it all happened so quickly. The DVD came out very quickly. I think they wanted to make the most of my popularity. I know I keep saying it but you never know when it will all end. It could be today, it could be tomorrow. One thing's for certain, though, it will end at some point.

Although the DVD was a really quick turnaround, I worked so hard on it. So hard, that by the end of the first two days I could barely walk. Serious.

As it happens the DVD didn't do quite as well as we had hoped. It wasn't a flop or nothing but it could have been bigger. Some things don't go major and again, you can't expect for everything to work all the time. I get that now, although at the beginning it used to worry me a lot! I think it didn't do as well because I was basically the same size. I was already really toned and had been going to the gym for ages. I think people like to see that dramatic weight loss, as it inspires them to do the same. If I can lose four stone in four months then people think they can too. The *Geordie Shore* lot – Vicky Pattinson, Holly Hagan and Charlotte Crosby – have all done phenomenally well and I think it's because they've had such drastic shape changes and on them you can see that straight away. Like, if Gemma lost about eight stone, then, perfect, that would work, but not for me because I was already the same size. I was known for being glam and that was my thing. When things don't work out, you do have to just pick yourself up and brush yourself down.

At the end of the day, I had an amazing time filming the DVD and I learned from it all. I also, even if you couldn't see it, got much fitter. I was out there with Claire and I was doing heavy training. It was such hard work. I knew I was doing it, but suddenly there was a massive amount of pressure on me to look a certain way. I put the pressure on myself. I don't want to look bad on a DVD, do I? I was worried for a while that I wouldn't be able to do a lot of the moves but I got my head down and I did it. I did two DVDs in two days! You see, everything I've done has been a challenge. Some are small and some are major, but I've overcome any worries and I've worked hard and done them. TV shows were the same. Can you imagine going on to live TV for the first time? It's bloody scary, I'm telling you. You just think: 'What the hell am I doing?' That's what I thought. One of the things I find hardest to get my head around is why people are interested in me. I'm not sure I'll ever totally understand. I think they relate to me and like the way I look, but I always worry about that and think I might wake up one day and no one will remember why they liked me!

Given how much I love my fashion and beauty, it was proper major to be given a gig on *This Morning* talking about beauty. It was so nerve-wracking, though. What if I stuttered? What if I said the wrong thing or I swore? It was all going round in my head. But again, I overcame the worries and I did it. I just talked about beauty stuff and I did a little feature about sparkles, so that you can, you know, have a bit of sparkle in your life. Don't be afraid of sparkles; they work on your legs and there's also sparkly nail polishes and all that. I talked about why having sparkle is such a good thing and why it makes you feel better. I had my cue cards to go through but I'm not sure I even looked down because I was just trying to get through the whole thing and do it well!

When I got home I watched it back over and over again, and I thought: 'Oh my god, I did well!' There's a few times that I did get myself in a bit of a panic and wonder why I was so nervous, but generally I think I did alright, and they asked me back so I can't have been that bad! I really enjoyed it. I was less nervous when it was Ruth (Langsford) and Eamonn (Holmes) presenting than I was with Holly (Willoughby) and Phil (Schofield). I think that's because I already knew Eamonn, and I think him and Ruth are great. I love them. Eamonn Holmes's daughter, Rebecca, lived with me for about a week. She stayed at my house when she was training to be a beautician and she came into the salon and did work experience. Eamonn sent me a note saying 'thank you' and he's always really appreciated what I did. Whenever I see them it's fun and I have a good time. They put me at my ease and whenever I go on *This Morning* they are lovely to me. She's so lovely Ruth, I really like her.

Anyway, back to *The Jump*. Sorry, I get distracted so easily and there's so much to tell. I don't know how I've crammed so much into the last six years. *The Jump* was, quite literally, me jumping back onto TV screens and putting me back in people's minds. I enjoyed the whole thing so much more than I could ever have imagined. Again, it was a learning curve, as being away from home for so long was a first for me. I'd never been away from Mum and Dad for that long and that was the bit that I was most worried about, really. But, like everything, if you get into the zone and stay focused you can do it, and I actually had great fun. That's always the way though: you're not looking forward to something and then you really enjoy it. I'm going to say it again but Tara Palmer-Tomkinson was brilliant. She's, like, in with the royals and all that. She's proper posh, but I loved her and we got on so well and she's mental fun. She'd be doing all these crazy things in the hotel and made us all giggle. I never have imagined that she'd be such a laugh and we'd still be friends now.

I went on quite a few reality TV shows but *The Jump* was, without a shadow of doubt, one of my favourites because I got to experience so much. I think I spent about £5k when I was over there buying champagne and treating everyone. I felt like me again, in a way…

I started to do a load of different reality shows like *Celebrity Super Spa* and *Dinner Date*, and they were all really good fun in their own way. They didn't all rate very highly, but that's not everything. On the *Celeb Super Spa* I had to teach them all vajazzling! Of course, I am the vajazzle queen, after all. *Super Spa* was quite a flop and I'd never do it ever again, but when they invited me to do it the first time I thought: 'Why not?' It was a surprise me being on the show because Arg was already on it and I was asked on to shock him. I get on quite well with Arg and so just before I came on they said to the rest of the celebrities: 'We've got an expert coming in today and she's the vajazzle queen. It's Amy Childs.' That was when I walked in and talked to all the girls and boys about vajazzling. It was quite fun and I really enjoyed it, but it was a total flop! I got on with Helen. She kept saying: 'You're so beautiful, you're amazing' and all that like. She wanted us to go on holiday and was saying: 'let's me and you go to Marbella' or 'we got to go away, me and you'. I'd only met her for, like, five minutes but we got along and she was hilarious – brilliant fun. There was all this talk about her and Arg while the show was going on and to tell you the truth, I wouldn't be surprised if I was a betting woman and all that!

Then there was *Dinner Date*. That was a right laugh and before I was asked do it I was a massive fan. Seriously, I absolutely love the show, it's probably my favourite show ever on TV. I've watched it for years and loved it from the beginning, and when I got that phone call, I didn't even have to think about it. I said '100% yes' straightaway, but

I asked if I would have to go out with them proper. No one ever properly goes on a date and ends up with the person, do they? I had a ball doing that show and I chose the right bloke.

I also did *Who's Doing the Dishes?* with Brian McFadden. See, I told you I did a lot of these kinds of programmes! I got on really well with Brian – he's a really nice guy – and before that I hadn't ever met him. He was a lot of fun. The idea of the show was that you get four people, a bit like *Come Dine With Me*, and they all come to your house and look through my house so that they can guess whose house it is. Kind of like that *Through the Keyhole* show. Of course, they guessed me straightaway because of the diamond chandeliers, leopard-print washing-up gloves, velvety sofas and all that stuff. That's just, like, SO me! Obviously I had to take all my pictures down so they couldn't have too many clues and then I had to make a dish so they could have a guess. I made a pear salad for starter (obviously because of my boobs), I then made a chicken with bright orange sauce which stood for my love of tan (LOL) and then I made jelly and ice cream (as in 'well jel'). So they got me straightaway. Obviously. It was such a fun show and Brian was a right laugh. I think his wife Vogue (Williams) is lovely too. I mostly saw Vogue on FaceTime when she was calling him. It was really sweet. We chatted a lot on that trip and he really opened up to me about everything. He's a nice guy and we've stayed friends since.

Being back in the press was fun, I hadn't been completely out of it but I had been doing a lot less as I already explained. I really enjoyed doing something other than business, as I'd been so busy with it and time had almost just passed me by. People, for some reason, had fallen in love with me when I did *TOWIE* and it was nice to know that they still had a soft spot after that break. I think I've done well, not only because I was the first person to leave *TOWIE* and set up a clothing range and a salon, but because I am myself. I can't cover up who I am, if I could I'd have stuck to what I was taught at those elocution lessons! Okay, ya! Nah, seriously, I'm just a young, fun girl. Even now I get excited that I'm on TV. I'm just me and I'll never lose that.

I started doing a column for a new magazine, *Child's Play*, and that's been really good too. It's in the mag every week and I get to talk about pretty much anything I want to. Anyone who reads that will know that I'm pretty normal. Back in May I went to Potters, where I've been going since I was three years old, with Brad. I pimped up one of those golf buggies with a 'well jel' number plate! Me and Brad, we were the youngest there by about 80 years and we were playing bingo and everything. I like getting away from it all sometimes and being in a really normal place. It brings back so many happy memories and makes me feel young again. It makes me feel like me.

## \*\*WINNING THE LIFE LOTTERY BUT LOSING MY MATES\*\*

You know what, I might have won the life lottery but I have lost along the way. I'm not asking for any sympathy. I've always been popular, I've always had a lot of friends, but with fame I lost a lot of my oldest friends and it's really bothered me. I've called this chapter 'Back to Reality' because sometimes that's how I feel at the moment. Not only am I going back to reality TV but I'm also finding ME again. You know, you might be riding high, but it's good to have a reality check and to make sure that you're not losing yourself along the way, because it's so easy to do. I see it all the time. My dad would never let me do that but it's sometimes very easy to let everything take over and to start believing your own hype. I'm not one of those types of celebs and so it's been hard that I've lost some of my mates. I mentioned earlier in the book about a few people who seemed uncomfortable with my fame, but when you are in the position that I'm in I think that it's important to have good friends around you, to keep you levelled, and these days I really know who those friends are. I have lost contact with so many people but there's one person I feel most sad about and that's Amy Chapman. Amy was my best friend from school and she doesn't talk to me anymore. I don't know why. I gave her a job and all that but maybe she's a bit jealous? She just cut me off. She worked as a nurse and then I gave her a job working for the Amy Childs Collection. I've not spoken to her for about three years now and she was my best friend. That sort of thing really upsets me. When I was younger I had a good friend Ella, who now has a baby. Ella was one of my best friends, but Amy was always the one that I confided in. She was the one that I was on the phone to at night. You get different kinds of friends, don't you? In school Ella was always with me, but Amy was my best friend. We did everything together, everything. You know, she was there for me. She was there for me when I went into *Big Brother*, and then suddenly she didn't want to know me anymore. I don't know why but I wonder whether she questioned my fame. I can't even remember what happened and then, all of a sudden, she just didn't talk to me. Her mum was best friends with my mum and they don't talk anymore either. It all just, like, happened. Totally random and proper upsetting. Those sort of things bother me.

Yeah, I've still got lots of friends, and I have a great family and Harry (lovely Harry), but I also worry about new people I meet and whether they want to be friends with me because of who I am rather than because they really like me. It proper killed me when Amy and I fell out 'cos we were so close. We had known each other since we were ten years old. We met at a disco, we were just dancing. She had a little bob and I had my hair all put up and I fell in love with her straightaway. I loved Amy. I was such a good friend to her and she was such a good friend to me. I thought about like texting her a couple of months ago asking if she wanted to chat. Sometimes I do feel a bit lost without her because she was always with me. Twelve years we were mates. I drove past her the other day and she looked at me, but there was nothing. As hard as it is, you don't need them people around you. You know, it's draining and it's upsetting. I'm emotional like that, though, and it bothers me. I can't help it. But that's a good thing, right?

Sorry, I don't mean to be all 'woe is me' and all that, it's just that I want to get across that no matter how big you get and no matter how well you do, feelings don't go away. If they do, you've been sucked into the world of showbusiness. And that's not me.

CHAPTER 6

# DOING BUSINESS THE AMY CHILDS WAY...

I'd like to think that I inject the fun factor into business. Meetings can often/always be dull. Talking about numbers can be a proper turn off, but if you do it my way you can have a lot of fun and be successful too. Business is hard but it don't have to be a total ball ache. It can, believe it or not, be enjoyable. Sit back, relax, pour a glass of prosecco and see how I do it...

## A DAY IN THE LIFE OF AMY CHILDS

So, I get up about 9am. I get up before that, actually, at about 8am, but I'm there on the phone straightaway. From the minute I'm awake I'm looking at all the news; you know, *Daily Mail* online, heatworld, *Daily Mirror* online, *The Sun*. I look at everything to see what's been going on, then I go on social media. I go on my Twitter, Instagram and Facebook to see what's going on and what's being said about everything, including me! At 9am I get up and sort the dog, Leon, out. Then I go to the gym. I always try to do a class in the morning and then proper work starts… after I get my hair and make-up done, obvs. If I haven't got a shoot or a meeting about the collection, I'll head down to the salon to see how things are going. Mum is mostly in the boutique, so I leave her to that as much as possible. The salon is where I'm needed most because I have a very clear idea of how it should work and how I want it to work. They are always busy, so if I can pop in to lend a hand, then I will. There are always a few meetings along the way but you can get through them, just remember to pack a nail file!

I've come a long way in the past six years. From working out of my mum's front room, I now have 15 members of staff in the warehouse, four in my boutique, five in the salon and four who work predominantly on growing the academy. It's pretty major, right?

## MY TOP TEN TIPS ON HOW TO BE SUCCESSFUL IN BUSINESS

1. Work hard. Hard graft will never let you down. If you get your head down and work hard, you will be rewarded. I'm proof of that and my parents are too. Look at what they've done and they didn't have fame or reality TV behind them, did they?

2. Confidence (believe in yourself). If you don't, how can you expect anyone else to believe in you and put faith in you? Have the courage of your own convictions. Keep your head held high and never let it drop. You are brilliant and you can succeed. Don't ever be lazy. If someone knocks you, pick yourself up and start again. You'll need to grow a thick skin if you want to go anywhere in the business world.

3. Organisation (never be disorganised). Meetings might be dull but don't be late for one. Tardiness looks like you don't give a damn and that's not a good first impression. Show off your knowledge and be prepared. I often have to write down little notes so that I don't forget things. Do your homework and don't rely on other people to do it for you.

4. Offer great service. If you offer rubbish service then people don't come back, no matter what industry that you are in. Fact. Make sure whoever your customer is that they loved their experience dealing with you and that they don't want to deal with anyone else. It's key to a successful start-up.

5. Find ways of making your business better and NEVER stand still. If you stay put and think you've got it licked then something will come back to bite you in the arse. You can always be better. Look at me, I am always trying to find new products, new treatments, new dress patterns. If you don't move with

the times and be ahead of the market then someone else will get there before you and it's game over.

6. Look at your market. Who are you appealing to? Have you identified the person that you want to buy your goods? Make sure you know who they are and what they want. If you get it wrong, then they won't come back.

7. Have the right business plan. Have you sat down and written a business plan? Do you know what you are trying to achieve and how you are going to go about achieving it? I find this sort of thing really hard, so I have to write everything down. Don't be embarrassed to do that. I have a business plan – what I plan to do with my businesses in the next two years, what I want to do with my collection and how I want to grow the companies. But don't be scared if something goes wrong or different to how you thought it would go. Like with me, if something doesn't work, you have to realise that and move on. Also, get rid of the dead stock. Just get rid of it and make some money back. Cut your losses early because everyone makes mistakes and everyone needs to make mistakes.

8. Stay focused and always find ways to improve your business. Do you know what you want? I always knew that I wanted my own salon and I've always focused on that. It wasn't the first thing that I did but I worked hard so that I could start it up. Make sure you know exactly what you want and never lose

sight of that. Be consistent in your thought process because if you lose sight of what you want, then it all gets a bit woolly. Consistency is key to making money in business. There will be lots of challenges on the way but if you stay focused on exactly what you want then it will become a reality.

9. Make sure that you have the right people around you. Look at me... there are so many things that I openly admit I'm crap at. In a meeting I find it hard to concentrate and I zone out really easily, but I have brilliant people around me to help and support me whenever I need it. It's so important. It's also important to be you. Don't ever pretend to be someone else. Being you is key to the success. If you're not you and pretend to be something that you're not then the façade at some point will drop and you'll be exposed for who you really are. Be proud of yourself.

10. Always look good. You know me, it's all about the way you look. Take care of yourself and take pride in how you look or how you turn up to a meeting because first impressions count, particularly in my industry. I think, no matter what you do, being glam is so important. I always look the part and that makes me feel confident. Confidence is absolutely key to being successful. If you don't feel right then you don't perform so well, for sure. If you don't look good, then you don't feel good. It's true.

## WHAT MAKE-UP TO WEAR
## FOR A BUSINESS MEETING

There seems to be a little bit of a rebellion at the moment when it comes to being fake – you know, like fake boobs and that. Lots of people seem to want to be natural all of a sudden and that's not easy, particularly if you're like me and you're not that natural (LOL), and you like dressing up and putting a heap of make-up on your face. But you need to know when it's right to pare it back, and a business meeting is one of those times. I have to remember this when I'm going to a meeting. I'm so used to making sure that I'm done right up so that the press can't pick me apart. I wear a lot of make-up and I always get my hair done before I step onto a red carpet. I absolutely love big hair. I love having hair extensions in at all times and that's why I choose Easilocks, because there is no damage to your own hair and they are a perfect match to my own natural colour. They are easy to maintain and I love Easilocks hair extensions! I think you can make a real statement with your hair, just not when you're going to a posh meeting!

Back to the red carpet. If you've got a bit of streaky tan, it'll be picked up on straightaway. You could be looking unbelievable but you've got something just a little bit out of place and that's what will be picked up on. I always think like that and I have to try and stop myself when I'm getting ready for a meeting because I'm not being judged in that room in the same way. I'm a great believer that you need to look your best but it shouldn't be over-the-top. Everyone can get it wrong (remember the bruised look I went in for?).

So, what you need for a meeting...

1. <u>Always</u> go for a professional look. Good appearance is key, so always groom your eyebrows and prep your skin. There's nothing worse than unruly eyebrows. The person you are in a meeting with is looking at your face the whole time and big, bushy, ungroomed eyebrows are going to be off-putting! Cleanse, tone and moisturise. No going to bed with make-up on the night before, or ever, actually, as it's so bad for your skin. The night before a big meeting make sure that you give your skin a really good clean and, oh my god, if you get a spot quickly whack some toothpaste on it. That's what I do and the spot goes pretty quickly. Taking make-up off and cleansing your skin is so important and make-up looks better and goes on much smoother when your skin is healthy and clean. So remember the night before you MUST cleanse, tone and moisturise. If you can you should try and have regular facials too. I know they can be a bit expensive but they are SO good for your skin. Exfoliation is even better because it's nice to have that fresh and dewy look. Everyone is into coconut oil at the moment, whether it's on their face or on their hair. It's supposed to be amazing but I worry

that it'll make my skin really oily and that I'll wake up looking like I've run a marathon!

2. Use a foundation that matches your skin colour. It's awful when you get that thick line along the bottom of your jaw. Stay natural, as less is more when it comes to business make-up. Simple, simple in the morning.

3. Eye make-up should be fairly neutral and definitely not bright or not smoky. No intense eyeshadow like you'd wear on a night out. Keep it classy. Put the eye make-up on the entire lid to make your eyes nice and wide.

4. Lips should be kept as natural as possible too. A nude lip looks professional. And NO lip liner. I love my lip liner and I do experiment with a lot of different lip liners, different bright colours or whatever, but not for a meeting it doesn't make for a good impression. If you can't bear to leave the house without it then wear a natural colour so that it can barely be seen. Make it fresh and long-lasting, you don't want to have to apply it over and over again.

5. Use mascara but don't put on great big false eyelashes. If you want to wear fake eyelashes then wear very subtle ones like my 'Flirt 1' range, but save the longer, more seductive ones like my 'Heartbreaker 1' and 'Heartbreaker 2' range for a night out. I've designed eight types of different false lashes and they are really popular. I loved designing them because you can wear them for all different occasions.

6. Only put on a little bit of bronzer. I love it, but bronzer is better suited for a night out.

7. Apply a little bit of blusher, but not too much. You don't want to look like a clown, just enough to make sure you look a bit lived in. Being as pale as a ghost ain't great.

8. I like to contour, it makes your cheekbones stand out and if it's done properly can be really effective. I often use the technique to try and bring out the best in my features. The other day I literally made my nose look skinnier by shading. It makes your face look more angular, I suppose. Anyone can do it but do it well. If you're not sure how then practice way before the morning you are planning to do it, as it can go horribly wrong. Contouring your face is like giving you a lot of shading and highlighting to your face. It really makes your face stand out, so when I go red carpet events I contour to the max. I use a MAC concealer, which is a lot lighter than my foundation. Don't go a little bit lighter, go WAY lighter. I use it on my cupid's bow, under my eyes and I put it down my nose and then do a darker fade on the corner of the nose. It's all about highlighting and shading, and it totally changes your face. It always needs to go on to emphasise your cheekbones and to accentuate features that are already there. I've got high cheekbones and I can make them look really high by just colouring in underneath. It's like doing a painting. I look in

the mirror and I've changed the way that I look. It's amazing. There's another brand that I use to contour as well, which is called Iconic London. It's got six palettes, from the lightest to the darkest colours, and when I'm contouring I use all of them. You wouldn't believe that I could use them all but I do. I use the lightest, which is, like white, and I use the darkest, which is, like brown for shading. Every girl loves contouring and Kim Kardashian is the queen of it. I love her. I've watched a load of YouTube videos to try and perfect how I contour and I think I've got it down a to a pretty fine art now…

You really have to be as natural as possible for a meeting. I would never go heavy. I know I do like my heavy make-up (just in case you hadn't noticed) but I would never go for smoky. Warm tones for the office, so more like browns, not blacks.

## THE PRODUCTS THAT I CANNOT LIVE WITHOUT

Everyone has their regulars in their make-up bag and I have a few that I swear by. Although I do try a lot of different products, I always come back to the trusty favourites! I LOVE MAC Sculpt foundation NC42. It's quite dark, but you know what I'm like with being pasty, I'm not that into the pale look and I like having something on my skin, just so I know it's on me.

I use Chanel Pro Lumière and I love Bobbi Brown. I use a lot of Bobbi Brown products when I'm contouring.

MASCARA: I love YSL false-lash effect because whenever I wear it people think that I have false lashes on. I've worn it for years and I won't change it.

BLUSHER: I love pretty much everything that MAC does, I'm a MAC girl, but I tend to use the Bobbi Brown highlighter pen instead of blusher. If I do ever wear blusher I prefer more peachy tones rather than big red rosy cheeks.

BRONZER: I use Bobbi Brown bronzer because it's excellent for contouring. It's called 'Deep'.

LIPSTICK/LIP GLOSS: I love a lip liner. I love Spice by MAC and I always wear it to make my lips look fuller. The lipsticks I use are Charlotte Tilbury lipsticks. They have SPF 15 in them and they are really long-lasting.

EYESHADOW PALETTE: I love the Naked 2 Palette by Urban Decay. It has some beautiful golds in there and it's good because it has colours for both daywear and eveningwear (when you can cake it on a bit).

And don't forget FACE PRIMER. I use face primer every morning before I apply my make-up because it holds everything in place and fills in any little blemishes that I have so that the other make-up glides on nicely. It also hydrates the skin and puts moisture back into your skin so that your make-up doesn't dry out. I use New CID because it has a nice scent and it's not too thick. I've even started to sell it in my salon.

## TANNING

I love a tan but don't do it yourself if you're going out to wow at an interview. The streaky look is pretty minging. I always say that you should definitely do it professionally. If you've got a major meeting, a big photo shoot, a red-carpet event or if you've got a big party, I would always say have a spray tan two to three days before, so that it's not too dark and looks that golden colour, nice and fresh.

Always exfoliate before you go for your tan so that you can avoid streaks wherever possible, and the next day you need to moisturise so that the tan really stands out and is a really nice healthy glow. Go more dramatic if you need to for a night out, but if you're after a job keep it classy. Don't do nothing too extreme. It's pretty bad going to a business meeting and being all caked in orange. That has happened to me before, just so you know. I remember it was much before *TOWIE* and I did a spray tan the night before a meeting, but, because I am trained to do spray tans, I tried out a few before I actually did it. I was experimenting with different spray tans. My hands were so orange and I couldn't get it off. It looked proper minging. There I was, a trained beauty therapist with orange hands and it looked well bad.

First impressions do count no matter what anyone says. If you turn up to a meeting or an interview and haven't bothered to make an effort it will show and the person interviewing you or looking to go into business with you will think that you don't care. I really do believe that.

I was talking earlier about my fake tan Amy Childs SprAmy (do you see what I did there?) and how I spent a long time creating it. I say the same to everyone – make sure you use a decent tan like mine. You don't want one that takes hours to dry or that is sticky. You don't want a tan that can't get to those hard-to-reach areas and you don't want a fake tan that doesn't look natural. You also need a colour guide so that it suits your skin. All my tans are a micro-fine mist spray that dries quickly, and they have a 360-degree spray pattern that allows you to get to those difficult areas. They also have a natural-tan guide colour that allows you to see where it has been applied. As a lover of the fake stuff I've tried to think of everything and I think I've nailed it. The scientific part ain't bad either. A lot of fake tans have parabens in them. Parabens are basically a preservative and there's been lots of chat about them not being good for you, so I've come up with a tan that is paraben-free and it contains Vitamin E and humectants (that's a moisturiser to you and me) for conditioning the skin, which I think is really important. If your skin is moisturised, then the tan takes better and looks better, for sure. My tans also have erythrulose (I know, another big word, sorry!). Basically the product works in synergy with DHA (an omega-3 fatty acid) to provide a long-lasting, even tan. So all-in-all it's pretty cool. You've gotta put the stuff on right but I swear by it and you won't go into a meeting looking like an orange.

The same goes for fingernails. Okay, so in the beauty industry it is a necessity, and I always clock* the hands and nails of people I'm interviewing. No one wants skanky hands massaging them or doing a pedicure. Fact. I look at their hands, of course I do, and you, as a customer, wouldn't be too happy if you had someone treating you with minging hands. It's not good. Your nails have to be immaculate for a meeting. Bitten is disgusting. I'm so on that. When I have girls here and they don't have very nice nails I do think twice, I'm not going to lie to you.

I know all these things can be pricey, but it's an investment in your future. You don't have to have long nails but even short, manicured nails look clean and tidy. I prefer a French manicure so that the nails are neutral; I'm not a fan of bright colours like pinks and I always have the white tips (I know it's plain but they look clean and professional). You'll never see my nails looking tatty. Even if you don't go to a salon, then give your hands a little manicure and paint them with a neutral polish. You don't have to be fancy or nothing. I love OPI colours. My favourite is 'Passion'. It's a beige-y, peachy colour, but it looks really fresh. Finish the whole thing off by using a nice hand cream so that you don't have dry skin and your hands feel silky smooth. I absolutely LOVE hand cream, and my favourite is The White Company's 'Flowers' because it smells so delicate. I like Clarins Hand and Nail Cream too. Whatever happens, you won't catch me walking out of the house without using hand cream. You should use it like you would a moisturiser and get in the habit of using it every day.

All of this stuff is part of a bigger picture and getting taken seriously. This is where I come into my own and properly know what I am talking about. If you look a bit daring and bright it might not hit the right note. Play it safe until you know what is acceptable.

## HOW TO GET TAKEN SERIOUSLY

1. Be glam but professional. 'Glam' doesn't mean that you have to have a face full of make-up. You can tone it all down and look nice and professional. When you walk into a meeting or interview you need to make sure the first impression is spot-on and hits the mark, no matter what the industry.

2. Look the person/people in the eye when you shake hands and give a firm handshake so that they know you mean business!

3. Don't over-talk. Answer questions and have your say but don't get off on listening to your own voice. Meetings can often be long and dull at the best of times, so don't make them go on longer than necessary!

4. Do your homework first. If you go into something without knowing what you are talking about then you could easily look like an idiot. I find business hard,

you know that, so I'm always writing little notes and making sure I understand everything beforehand.

5.  Listen. I always try and learn something from every meeting that I go to. Mum has always taught me that and I'm still doing it. Listen to what people have to say. I have a habit of drifting off and getting easily distracted and that ain't good but try as hard as you can to listen and if you're not sure of something don't be afraid to ask. Sometimes I think I'm being stupid and don't want to ask, so I write it down and ask someone about it after! I'm getting better at asking questions and listening to what people are saying and I am learning so much.

## HOW TO DRESS CONFIDENTLY OR FOR A BUSINESS MEETING

If you don't look the part how are you expected to actually be the part? You need to make people believe that you know what you are talking about and that you have the confidence to deliver. Private school helped me to handle myself, and I've got better as time has gone on and the more tricky situations that I've been in.

Everyone gets it a bit wrong sometimes, but remember to style it out. I did when I went to the TV BAFTAs. Me and Harry were presenting an award and I wanted to look my best; I bought myself a Victoria Beckham dress, I don't think I've ever spent so much money on a dress before, it was about

£2,500 I think, but I loved it and I still do, despite what I'm about to tell you! So just before I left, as Jade was doing my dress up, she caught her finger on the zip. She had cut it and blood was literally pouring out onto the dress. She was proper mortified and as much as we tried to get the blood off the dress it wouldn't go away. As we were wiping the dress and pouring water over it, it was getting more and more smudged and pinker and pinker, but the blood wasn't going. Jade was crying, I was screaming, but there was nothing we could do, it was too late to change my dress and the show had to go on! Mum was there too, and she was doing all the things that she could think of but it was stained and that was that. So I went onto the red carpet wearing the dress but keeping my hand over the stain. It was just on my left butt cheek and I literally spent the whole time with my hand over it, like I was posing. If my hand wasn't over it then Harry, who was with me was covering it with his! Go on, look at the pictures and you can see that in every single one I have my hand over the patch on my backside. It's well funny, but it wasn't at the time. That was the first time, I think, that I've ever got it wrong, although that was out of my control! I styled it out, though, and that's the main thing because no one ever noticed!

Even before *TOWIE* days I've never ever got it wrong with my clothes or my make-up and even my hair. Never. Because I've always been glam, I've always spent time planning and thinking the night before about what I should wear, what should my jewellery be like and my hair and make-up. I always knew before I went to bed what I'd be wearing the next day. Sometimes, less is more. It's hard for me to take my own advice on that, but it's true. Don't go 'edgy' because you will feel awful and it will show in the way that you come across. Dress confident and you will feel confident. I really believe that.

Anyway, make sure you dress sophisticated for meetings. No one wants to see a glamour-model look. A nice, fitted dress and a jacket is perfect. I have got loads in the collection that look really smart and that, with a jacket, really professional. Or a nice pencil skirt with a blouse and blazer or a nice little cardigan would work, but do NOT wear a top that shows off a lot of cleavage. Separates can work too, and I've designed a few really cool outfits that would also be suitable for a professional situation. Team it with some nude heels and you'll look the part. Dress stylish and make sure it's flattering for your body. Like, always wear an over-the-knee skirt or dress to give a good impression and absolutely NO over-the-knee boots. I love Louboutins because they look smart no matter what, but I know they aren't exactly affordable. There are loads of different shops that offer cheap alternatives, like New Look or even Primark. Oh, and keep the jewellery simple too. You don't need to wear in-your-face necklaces, instead just wear a thin gold chain or a statement watch and nothing else. I don't think that you need a watch, a bracelet, a necklace, rings etc. Choose one thing and keep it basic.

Obviously, on a night out it's a whole different ball game and you can glam it up all the way. Take all the time you need to get ready for a night out. I love the getting-ready and dressing-up part. It's almost the best bit! Same principle as before a meeting, though: don't fake tan on the same day as you're going out or it will look a total mess and streaky. On a night out, though – you don't have to think toned-down, you can go all-out on the glam front. A bit of a booby dress or top, something short and some really high heels. There's nothing better than getting dressed up and glam. Get your hair done. I have mine washed and blow-dried once a week and it lasts me, I just use my sleep-in rollers from my collection. They are glittery, obviously, which means I look glam even with my rollers in and give me big, bouncy hair! My sleep rollers have been a huge success for me. It was at one of the clothes shows that I met a lady producing them and I chatted to her about designing my own range and that's what we did. They have been so successful and I promote them by wearing them down the salon and still they sell really well. Leopard print, sparkles – those sleep rollers are so me! I'll often pop down to Tesco in them or go shopping in them! I don't care if they are sleep rollers, they look great! Wash, dry and pop in the rollers and it'll look like you've been in the hairdressers all afternoon! I LOVE big hair, the bigger the better on a night out. Backcomb it, hairspray it (Elnett is my favourite!), do whatever you need to make that hair big! Don't do that, though, if you are going for a meeting or an interview. I'm not sure the big hair look is what people want see in a situation like that, as much as I love it!

## BUSINESS-MEETING HAIR

Okay, so we all know that I love BIG hair. Have I said that enough yet? Usually, I can't get enough volume into my hair but for a business meeting you need to resist. Don't do it. You need to look professional and have a slicked-back ponytail or a nice little bun or a topknot or a French plait. Any of those will work but personally I do think that it needs to be up. I still like those big buns; they still look classy and elegant, and, anyway, a bun is 'in' at the moment. Obviously, if you have it short, it's harder, but then it's much easier to give it a little blow-dry yourself and make it look smart. You need to look fresh. Seriously, make sure your hair isn't down or you might look a bit glamour-model again and if you're nervous you don't want to have anything to distract you and that makes you want to play with it. If my hair is down, I know I'm always flicking it and running my fingers through it. It's a subconscious, nervous thing, I think. I always think hair that's neatly tied back looks professional and clean and tidy. In my business that stands for a lot. As with the nails, the same goes for hair – if you are getting a massage or having a manicure, you don't want the person doing it to have their hair all over their face. You want them to look neat and tidy. It's the professional look and you've got to look the part.

## TAKE CARE OF YOURSELF

I pride myself on taking care of myself. I like to look my best even if I don't actually need to and I think that it's really important to look after yourself.

I go to the gym about three times a week but I'm not stick-thin, I'm curvy (I think). I'd hate to be, like, a skinny little thing. I don't think it's attractive at all. I'm a normal girl and I like my Chinese takeaway and my glasses of wine, and I think that's important. Can you imagine being one of these people that starves themselves of all the nice things? I can't imagine a world without a packet of Twiglets. That'd be bang out of order*. I have to eat quite healthy because of my job and what I do, but I'm not some kind of skinny Minnie. Behave*.

I've talked a lot about making sure that you are surrounded by the right people and I am really lucky that I have my family and my management that look after me. 100%. But I've also got another secret weapon and that's Abby...

I literally could NOT live without Abby. She pretty much lives at my house and looks after me. You know I can't really cook, right? I can do fajitas and homemade pizza but that's literally it. Well, Abby helps me with all that, along with everything else! Abby is an Amynator. That means a big Amy Childs fan. Basically, she was at the salon, like, every time I was in there and we just got talking most of the time that I went in, and I loved her. She was looking for a Saturday job and she asked me if I could help her. She always used to be so helpful when she was in, asking if she could help out with things and make tea for the clients. She never just sat there like other fans might, she used her confidence to make me take notice, and I did, so I gave her a Saturday job. At first she was cleaning up for me and all that, but that's nothing to be ashamed of. She's been working her way up and almost teaching herself on the job. She is learning how to manage a successful business and manage a team of people. Seriously, everyone needs an Abby in their lives. She is amazing. Even Hannah at the salon thinks so! Abby still works for me on a Saturday; she'll cover the reception in the salon, and then she goes to the boutique and works there. She's like a junior Amy Childs!

Abby studies beauty anyway, so she can do nails and all things like that, and it's great practice for her in the salon to see how it all works.

I think Abby thinks I'm really funny. She gets to see everything: the good, the bad and the ugly! She's seen me lose it because I've run out of spray tan in the house or because we've run out of wine in the fridge! Or when I haven't got a bag of Twiglets in the cupboard. She's seen it all! I think she finds it interesting, in a way. Abby pretty much lives here and she'll often cook for me and Brad because I'm so useless at it. She sees the good times and she sees the bad times. It's been a learning curve for poor Abby! She gets well upset when the haters are on one. I might be used to the problems I get on social media but it makes Abby mad! She's like: 'Oh my god!' when she sees people being bang out of order about me.

She is still pretty innocent because she hasn't grown the thick skin I have when it comes to the comments yet. She doesn't understand how people can judge me when they haven't even met me. She's right, but it bothers her way more than it does me these days.

Abby gets to see everything too, like with Brad. No one knew about him until earlier this year but Abby did! She thinks he is lovely and that he's really good for me because he looks after me and we actually get on (and we don't often row). Abby says that she sees us laughing together all of the time and she likes to see me happy. Me and Brad, we aren't big going-out sorts, so Abby sees us at home chilling out mostly and she sees that we get on like an old married couple! She's seen my ex-boyfriends so I do take Abby's opinion and she says that in the past she's never imagined me ending up with the person I've been seeing, but with Brad, Abby thinks it's different. She thinks we will stay together and that this is the one! Personally, I think me and Brad are a good team and, besides, he has the same OCD as me and is always cleaning! Between me, Abby and Brad the house is always spotless!

So Abby started working on a Saturday with me in the salon and then when I went away and I needed someone to look after Leon she offered. That was it, really. She pretty much moved in! I'm away quite a lot with work so it's brilliant to have her around to look after everything for me when I'm not about. I think Abby is pretty much here every day except for weekends when she goes home to her family! She doesn't live far away, near Lakeside, so only about 15 or 20 minutes away. It works well, I think, and she likes the freedom of living at mine and I love having her around. She is brilliant and she makes a great cup of tea! That's very important to me, given the amount that I drink! Abby doesn't have to clear up or anything for me, my OCD makes sure of that! Probably even Abby had a different opinion of me until she got to know me. But I'm a good person. I'm a kind person and although I've been successful I wouldn't jeopardise anything for fame and I mean that. I'm not just saying it because I'm in a good position now but I genuinely do mean it. You get used sometimes if you're like me, but I'd rather be like that and be able to sleep at night than be fierce and hard with people. Abby has become my resident angel, receptionist, dog whisperer, cleaner and chef. You name it, Abby is all over it! She does everything, my little Amy Childs fan. Abby is the best.

I got done for speeding not so long ago (I'm not proud of myself) and I had to go on one of these speed-awareness courses. The day before I'd been out all day, I was in Manchester all that day and I didn't get home until 1:45am. When I got back, Abby's there and she's got me totally organised for the next day. She'd got all the paperwork out for me and found my passport, which I needed. She'd literally got everything organised. When I got upstairs, she'd cleaned my bath for me and cleaned it all underneath. I don't ask her to, she just does it. She'd hoovered upstairs. Brad's stuff is in a pile and she's ironed it all. Brad's stuff, not mine. How amazing is she? But Abby thinks that she is living the dream. When she showed up each week at my salon she just didn't want to take 'no' for an answer. She was a huge fan of mine and she had the biggest Amy Childs fan page out of everybody I'd met. She had about six thousand people following it. At first I was like: 'Let's give Abby a job', because I really admired her persistence. I think that's a really good way to be with people. Now Abby is pretty much living with me and she honestly thinks she is living the dream! I suppose she is a bit like my very own PA these days and I don't know what I'd do without her. Abby is the one who half the time gets me where I need to be on time and with what I'm supposed to have with me!

Other than all the business *stuff* that I've done, have launched and am working on, I do various different endorsements too. And, again, when I go to meet the companies who are potentially looking for me to do some work for them I am very aware of how I need to look and I carefully plan my outfit. I think it's probably all in the planning, actually, and if you do plan the whole outfit, right down to the final detail, you feel so much better and more confident. I know I do.

In fact, I've been paid to do a fair few endorsements over the years and they've all been fun in their own way. I've listed them all below because I don't suppose you remember a lot of them? I had to really think about it so that I could remember all of them myself! There's been a real variety and it gives you some idea of how you shouldn't really say 'no' to things when they are offered to you. Start becoming a snob about jobs and the wheels will start to come off. I'm not saying you have to say 'yes' to everything but if you're considering saying 'no' then make sure that it's for the right reasons…

## MY ENDORSEMENTS FROM THE BEGINNING OF THIS INCREDIBLE JOURNEY….

1. Lipsy Limited: 2010
2. Caprice Valentine Lingerie: December 2010
3. Barclaycard: June 2011
4. Alton Towers Resort: June 2011
5. Philips: June 2011
6. Comet PLC: June 2011
7. Ultimo: October 2011
8. *Get Up and Dance* (for Nintendo Wii, PlayStation Move for 9. PlayStation 3): November 2011
10. BABTAC: December 2011
11. Fake Bake: 2012
12. Kandee Shoes – Pink Lemonade: 2012
13. Walkers: January 2012
14. Lonsdale: January 2012
15. Samsung Smart Camera: April 2012
16. Nature Valley Games: June 2012
17. Sleep-in Rollers: November 2012
18. Annabelle's Wigs: November 2012
19. Carphone Warehouse: November 2012
20. Everything Everywhere and Saatchi & Saatchi: January 2013

21. Bathstore: February 2013
22. Yummypets: June 2013
23. Alexis Smith Lingerie: June 2013
24. Splendid Communications – MoneySuperMarket:
    September 2014
25. RNIB (Royal National Institute of the Blind):
    November 2014
26. Silk'n: 2014

I've always been the same when it comes to wanting to work and be something. I never really thought that much about what people were saying about me becoming famous and all that, but even from an early age (before the boob job) the writing was on the wall, I think.

At 14 years old I modelled for L'Oréal. My hairdressers sent a picture of me off to them and before long I'd had a call asking me to model for them, it was a big campaign in Chelmsford that they were doing. Of course, I did it. The pictures make me cringe a bit now! You can see a load of snaps of me over the years in this book. Enjoy them, because, as you'll see, I have changed quite a lot! Do you even recognise me?! 😉

## CHAPTER 7

# WHAT'S NEXT?

I have literally come SO far in such a short space of time. There's barely been a moment to breathe. My life since I was 19 years old has been, like, a whirlwind and it's been amazing.I've achieved more than I ever thought possible when it comes to business, but that doesn't mean I need to stand still. If I do life will pass me by and I'll get lost along the way. I'd like to keep this dream alive as long as I possibly can and, just like with the salon, me and Hannah are looking for new things to try, or Claire and me are always trying to find the next best dress design. I have to think about what I want from my future and what I can do to make sure that I don't fall down one of these days like so many have before me. I might have enough to live a comfortable life on but I want the best for whatever my future holds and being successful is the key to having an even better life.

As I write this it's still going pretty damn well TBH. I'm not arrogant enough to think that this will last forever. That would be really nice and I'm going to give it a damned good shot. I always try and do everything as right as possible, like invest the money in bricks and mortar, and make sure that I'm not throwing it all away.

As you know by now, family is everything to me and having a family of my own is definitely something that I want. I'm going to be really honest, I wouldn't put money or fame before that. I'm lucky to have done as well as I have at my age and every day is a blessing, but having a family of my own is another dream that I would like to come true in the not-too-distant future. Is Brad the one? I think he probably is, although I'm not sure my mum wants to hear that! Mum hasn't always liked my boyfriends and she worries about all this stuff all of the time. She's like any mum and wants the best for her daughter and I get that. I know it's hard because I'm successful in my own right and Mum wants me to meet someone who will look after me and treat me like a princess. She worries about me being used, but that sort of thing doesn't bother me because I know that I've been very careful with my money and I've not just thrown it away. Apart from the boyfriends, she's probably my biggest fan, even with everything that's gone on in our lives.

Despite everything, none of us have changed and we won't. We're still the same normal family. I think the thing is that we've all stayed really normal, and I know I'm looking to move somewhere bigger, but I'm not one of these in-your-face, flashing-the-cash kind of people. I couldn't even tell you what's in my bank account. I'm happy if I can afford to get my nails done every three weeks and my hair done

once a week. Those are the things that make me happy.
Mum says she's always had to fight off the boys from me,
so she's always been really strict. People used to say to her
that I will marry a footballer and that, and she says she
can remember seeing my brother Billy's mates looking at
me. When I was, like, sixteen the older boys started to get
interested and Mum wasn't happy about it! As she got older
and I started to get boyfriends, Mum and Dad never let them
stay over.

I think Mum really wants someone who's on a little bit
of my level career-wise. Mum doesn't think it works in a
relationship if you've not got the same outlook and that. Dad
was always the earner in our house, paying the mortgage and
all that, but if he went through bad times she'd always be
there supporting him. I think she sees their relationship as a
team and she wants me to find that with someone. Mum says
her money was her own, though, and she could spend it how
she wanted to, whether it was treating me and Billy or going
on a holiday because Dad had all the rest covered and I don't
think she wants all the pressure to be on me. I do get that but
I'm happy right now. It doesn't worry me that Brad isn't on
my earning level or whatever, because he is on my thinking
level and it's so hard for me to meet someone like that now
that I have met someone who treats me right I don't want to
give it up.

Mum probably worries that my want for a family will affect
the career that I've worked so hard for, but I really do believe
that women can do both. It shouldn't be a choice for women,

they should be able to be successful in their career and have a family and I think mums working hard, like my mum did, sets a really good example for their children. I love the idea of being able to tell my kids about how I've got to where I've got. I think it will drive them to try their best and to be successful too. I know working and being a mum ain't gonna be easy but I'm sure it's easier in my position than it is a for a lot of people. Just like we change up the dresses and come up with new ideas, if I were to have a family why couldn't I design a range of maternity wear? Just because you're baking a baby doesn't mean that you can't be glam, that is for sure. I've spoken to loads of different mums about maternity wear and they all say that they lived in comfy leggings and flowery smock tops, but I've got loads of really smart ideas to change the face of the whole maternity-clothing thing. You might be big but why look dowdy? I think a lot of women would welcome something like that, don't you? And I don't think there's any need to have to suddenly dress like an old woman! No way. It's an exciting time so look excited in what you are wearing. I'm not saying I'm about to go and have a baby but at some point I do want one and it's always good to think about adapting businesses and making provision for the future.

Brad supports all these ideas of mine and listens to me going on about them, that's why it's easy. I'm a normal girl and he's normal boy. I'm so normal that I still get excited about meeting all the old boy bands. I've gotta tell you something that's really funny. The three Bs: Blue, Busted and Blazing Squad – well, I used to love them. I was such a massive fan it was ridiculous, so here's the story. Lee Ryan was my favourite out of Blue because he was the best looking and I'd been to nearly all the Blue concerts but I'd never got to meet any of them. So, I'm out of *TOWIE* by this point and I'm getting to meet celebrities. It was amazing and every time that I was at a party with a celebrity I used to think: 'how have I managed this?!' I saw Emma Willis once and was like: 'Oh my god, I was the biggest Busted fan!' I was so sad but I was so excited that I was meeting these people! I told her that I'd met Matt once when I was younger but that I had become so excited that I'd started to cry! Mortifying. She told me that she couldn't wait to tell him. Can you imagine? Anyway, I'm doing what I always do and I'm going off the point. So after all those years of loving Lee Ryan, when I came out of the *CBB* house he called me and he was like: 'Alright Ames?' and I was like: 'Who's this?' and he was like: 'It's Lee Ryan from Blue' and I was like: 'Oh my god, it's Lee Ryan! You alright?' I got a bit nervous, to tell you the truth, and he told me that he was ringing because he knew that I was a fan. I think he was a bit drunk, TBH, but he was saying he wanted to take me out. He was probably asking everyone out but I was just happy to be talking to Lee Ryan! I was on the phone to him for half an hour and he was asking me all of these questions about *TOWIE* and asking me why I'd left. It was so random. He said the show wasn't the same without me! I couldn't believe that he even watched it! I was in such shock I can now barely remember what I said to him, but when I got off the phone Mum asked me who it was. I went: 'It was

Lee Ryan, he rang me out of the blue.' And that was it, she was cracking up laughing at me. Geddit? Lee Ryan ringing me out of the Blue! I didn't even know what I had said but Mum was killing herself laughing. LOL. Then I rang Hannah to tell her that he'd called and I was crying because it was so funny. I couldn't get my words out. So there you go.

For five years my life hasn't stopped and it's been amazing but as much as I say that it would be nice at some point to slow down a bit and chill, I can't see that happening, though. I'll never give up on my businesses, I will always give them 100%. I like to keep moving so I never get bored.

When I do have children, though, I hope I'm like my mum. I'll probably be every bit as protective. She always did her best for us, no matter what, from going without so that we could have something we wanted or needed, to being the mum who welcomed everyone in. As I got older my mates would always be 'round my house. Even when I got a lot older and went to the pub, my mates would come in after and my mum wouldn't mind at all, she'd ask them to stay overnight! She loved having a bustling house, I think, and also she preferred having everyone over and knowing where I was. I want to be like her when I grow up. She is my role model and if you've got a strong one of those you'll never go wrong.

The thing with Mum is she still can't really believe how things have turned out, but that's because she's normal. She came back from the boutique the other day and she was all hot and red and she was so excited because she'd sold, like, a hundred bottles of my perfume. Every week when a *TOWIE* tour rocks up we sell about that amount, but it still surprises Mum. She still can't get over it and comes home and is really excited about it. Don't get me wrong, she's right, it's pretty amazing and I'll never take it for granted. Perfume was one of the things that I told Claire at the very beginning that I wanted to do. I always dreamed of having my very own perfume and, in August 2012, I was able to do it.

Being able to create your own perfume is so much fun. I was basically creating something that I wanted to wear. It was completely tailored to what I like and it's definitely my perfume of choice. I LOVE it.

I was really involved with creating the perfume, right from going into the labs and testing it and checking that it was right, to making sure the bottle was how I wanted it and that the packaging screamed Amy Childs! There were a lot of alterations I had to make at first, for instance it was too strong and then I thought it didn't last long enough. I needed to be sure that the perfume was exactly right. I had to get the right mix or it wouldn't do well.

I've actually created two perfumes now. My latest one came out last year and, although it has the same name, it is really quite different. The first one was *me* when I was younger, I suppose. I'm still fruity and sweet but back when I created that I chose something that was a nod to me as a person.

I expect you know all about top notes and bottom notes and all that random stuff but it took me a while to get on board and learn about it all. My first perfume was, as I mentioned, sweet and fruity. I LOVE pomegranate and I've always loved the Jo Malone Pomegranate scent, so that was definitely going in because that is one of my favourite smells. So, it has top notes of exotic fruits and pomegranate, as well as top notes of fresh green leaves, because I like everything to be fresh. Also central to the perfume is a floral smell, which is made up of lotus, champaka and purple orchid. And then amber, skin musk, vanilla and soft woods form the base notes of it.

Honestly, it's gorge, and it came in a lovely pink bottle. It sold really well but, again, like with everything else, I couldn't stand still and I needed to bring out a new one. Both of them add a real glam finish to whatever you are wearing. Glam is at the heart of everything… for me, anyway.

My most recent perfume comes in a different-shaped purple bottle. It's kind of smoother and perhaps more sophisticated. I guess I wanted to change it up. I'm a bit older and so my tastes have changed a little. It's still very me but it has a more grown-up feel/smell about it. I had no idea about what went into producing your own perfume before but it's really fun to get to make something that is exactly what you like. This one is a very floral fragrance with the top note of neroli (an essential oil from the blossom of a bitter orange tree). It has middle notes of tiare flower and the base note is palisander rosewood, which gives it the more woody tone.

As with all the other stuff I have in my range, I have taken it all over the country to promote it and going forward I want to do even more of that. I'd really like to start franchising the Amy Childs brand. Basically what that means is that people would be able to get my products from their own local high street, because there'd be branches opening all over the country. Or at least at first having concession stands in other stores. I know people can get all my goodies online but it's sometimes nice to be able to go in and browse and unless you live in or around Essex it's really hard, almost impossible, for people to do that. Hannah and I talk about franchising the salon too. I think, because I've got the Amy Childs Academy up and running now (although, I do want to grow it), it will mean that we are getting more and more people trained up to my standard, and I'd like to see those people employed in salons all over the country. I'm sure that in the north of England it would go down really well with people. Like, at the moment, people and fans go to Newcastle to see all the different *Geordie Shore* sights, but I'm sure that if there was an Amy Childs salon that it would be equally popular for people. I think the idea has got real potential and that's something I'm looking into doing. Definitely. It's one of those things that we talk about and just haven't actioned. I need to get on with it. There's lot of hoops to jump through, though, before it can all happen and percentages to split between people before business deals can be done. I don't really understand it (I really do struggle to understand these sorts of things), but this is where Claire comes in and she makes sure that it's the best deal for everyone involved. I know that it will happen but I'd like to see it become a reality sooner rather than later.

I'm really excited about the doors that the academy opens for us. Last January I did a talk at Stafford College.

It is always nerve-wracking doing those talks to a load of students but, although I was crapping myself beforehand, as soon as I got in there I was okay. So at Stafford College, loads of beauty students turned up to the talk and I wanted to make them believe in themselves, to make them believe that they, too, can be successful.

I'm always honest with people and I tell the students how hard parts of the business are to me, but I think that honesty helps them to have even more confidence that if I can do it, then so can they. Stafford College actually want to have their own Amy Childs Academy, so that the students will learn my way, with my products. It's going to be brilliant because it'll be a course and they'll include teaching them all about my brand and how you can get a brand as big as I have, as well as how to get those products into a high-street store. I wouldn't have known without having the people around me that I do and this way it gives other people, who don't necessarily have my original platform, a chance to learn too, and build their dreams. I want to do more of this and get into as many places as possible. At the end of the course they will be a qualified beautician and also have a qualification in fashion. Isn't it amazing?

It's strange for me these days because I feel a certain amount of pressure to be this businesswoman, but I'm still just Amy Childs. I struggle with that a lot because in my head they don't really go together. Most people of my age don't have the same pressures as I do. I'm not complaining at all but there is obviously certain pressure to make sure that everyone is paid on time and correctly and all that. My businesses need to do well, as people rely on me and that's a big deal. All the girls are on different wages and some of them are on commission, so they get more if they sell the different products and it can really vary from one month to the next. One week I'll be asking them all to try and sell the 3D Lipo course, and it's up to them to try and do that. I'm not a hard boss, as I mentioned before, but I do like to see that things are done properly and when I was in the salon not so long ago a lady said that she'd left a message and that no one had got back to her. That doesn't make me very happy because that's how you lose customers and I can't afford to do that. I rang the lady back and offered her free 3D Lipo as an apology. I'd never have forgotten to call people back when I was working in the salon with Sharon and there's no way that she'd let me forget either. That's one of the first rules: customers are always right (although it might not feel that way at times). It's important that I get the girls working in the salon as I would if I were there. I feel very passionate about that and Sharon would never accept second best. Once one customer is dissatisfied then it can have a snowball effect; they will talk to someone else and so it goes on. When I first take people on I try and instil some of those values, but I think people who will do the Amy Childs courses through the academy will be on it already.

At the moment I hold meetings about their hair, make-up, everything because I know for a fact that when I worked at

Sharon's I was always immaculate. I was always perfect and there was never a hair out of place and that's how I like my girls to be. Sharon has made me the boss that I am because I watched her every day for two and a half years. I studied how she was with clients, how she was in herself and how she was as a boss, and when I walk in to that salon I go straight back to how I was when I worked with her. I go in and say: 'right, who wants a cup of tea or coffee?' I haven't got to do that anymore but I do it because I know no different. This lady said to me: 'I can't believe you're making me a tea' but, of course, I'll make a tea for anyone. As I've said before, don't get too big for your boots because it'll all go wrong. And besides, I make a good cuppa!

I'm not so good at the business side, though, as in all the numbers and that. Definitely not. Claire is so good because she knows how all the financial things and figures work. You can't be good at everything but you can have good people around you, like I do. The overall company is called Dolly Diamond and it makes sense for us two. I'm the dolly at the desk, looking all glam and making sure everything is being done properly (or the dolly wearing all the dresses), and Claire is the diamond master minding the whole thing! I'm the dolly and Claire is the diamond. I can't do what she does and she can't do what I do. That's why it works. Claire is straight to the point and gets the job done and I like to chit-chat and have a bit of banter with people, saying things like: 'Hi girls, you okay? Come in! So, girls, we've got a few treatments here today. I've got a pedicure, manicure and two appointments.

What do you want?' I love all that. We play to our strengths. I do try and understand things, I really do, and I'm definitely getting better, but there are still things now, such as with the house where I wonder what I'm doing and get a headache.

My mum helps me and I've got an amazing manager, and an accountant who sits down with me to explain things. I sit there and try to take it all in and then I go home and think about it some more, so I can try to understand. I can't always avoid meetings and expect other people to do it. Not so long ago I had to go to a meeting that was, like, four hours long. Groan. It was about a college buying in my tan to use with all the training, which is amazing. But four hours for me is a long time in a meeting and I did have a headache by the end just trying to understand what everyone was saying and all that! You can imagine what I was thinking; my mind kept wandering on to other things and at the same time I was giving myself a little talking to, like: 'Ames, you're in a meeting. Concentrate!' But my head was screaming: 'Get me out of here!' I do my best by sitting there and trying to take in as much as possible.

I can remember the first meeting I ever went to. We were talking about the business. It was actually on my TV show and everything. They filmed me sitting in the bank in this meeting not having a clue and the producers loved it. I was looking at all the other girls and I wasn't really concentrating, but that's what people loved about me. Because when it comes to numbers I just glaze over. Not because I don't want to know, I just really don't understand it. It really hasn't been easy for me and because of my dyslexia it has been even harder.

Life isn't always fair and I thought this the other day when I won at the dogs. I won, like, £2,500 after putting a £200 bet down. It hit me then that that wasn't really fair. I don't need the money, why was I winning so much when someone else could have needed it more? But once you have the money you can take more risk with it and gamble a bit more. I was willing and able to lose that money, whereas someone else might have only been able to put a tenner on and their pay-out would have been less. Hope you know where I'm coming from.

I am a lucky person but you make your own luck sometimes too. I really do think that. And you can change your fortune too. I wasn't independent at all before I moved out but once I did move out I realised a lot of things about myself that I hadn't realised before. For instance, I didn't know that I'm very organised with work. I like to write myself notes and I can't live without a diary with everything that I have to do written down in it. I love a checklist. I like to tick them off as I go, it feels very satisfying. I have to be organised because I have so much on. One way or another, I need to know what I'm doing. Which is why I get all my clothes ready the night before.

I mentioned earlier that I'm putting all my money into property. At 25 years of age, I own three houses and I'm just about to buy my fourth! Of course, I'd never shout about them, but you know what I mean. You don't have to shout the loudest to earn the most, okay. I'm investing in properties so if it all goes wrong tomorrow I have something to fall back on, and that's the bottom line really.

I know that some people who know that I'm successful expect me to pretty much pay for everything when we go out and that but my mates don't take this mick out of me, and if I go out with my parents I always forget my wallet so my dad has to pay! I'm a pretty generous person, although my mum calls me the queen because I never have my purse or any cash on me!

I know that I've touched on it before, but how do you see if people are only in it for the money? It's really hard to know and that's why I feel so settled and happy with Brad. He's a bit of me* because he genuinely isn't interested in the whole fame thing and making money. He gives me money, like an allowance, each week if he's staying at mine. It's not the other way round and this is the first time that this has ever happened for me. It's so easy to get swept up and seduced by everything around me but that doesn't make a relationship work. What makes it work is when you have banter in the evenings and can have a right old laugh at the same thing. My mum and dad love each other no matter what, and my mum always says that even when she put on a load of weight and said to dad she'd have a gastric band, he was like: 'No way. I love you how you are.' That's well sweet. They've been together for, like, 18 years and I want that, I really do. And I think, in Brad, I've found it. Yes, we row, but what couple doesn't?

Mum worries that if I'm with someone and have kids with them and they don't have their own money that it will be me supporting them all our lives. I do get what she means and I can see how a mum would feel like that, but we're not living in the dark ages now. Women can be the bigger earner and the kind of guys I'm attracted to aren't the kind that work earning a ton of cash in the city.

I've fallen in love with somebody who isn't bothered by my fame, who isn't interested in my fame. There, I've said it… I've completely fallen in love with Brad. He sees me, Amy Childs, and he's so relaxed and chilled out that it helps me to get everything into perspective too.

I was asked the other day what I'd like to do next, apart from grow my businesses, and there's a part of me that really enjoys doing all the broadcast stuff. I love doing *This Morning* and the beauty segments and all that. I also did Kiss 100 radio the other day and I loved it! It got me thinking… maybe I should become like a radio DJ or something? That would be well funny. Perhaps that should be my next project! What do you reckon? I've been banging on about how everything is possible if you put in the effort, so maybe!

One thing's for sure in all this madness and craziness. One thing I can guarantee 100% before I leave you is that I'll always be me, Amy Childs, and I will NEVER change. I will always be the little girl who loved her dollies and liked to dress up in her mum's heels. I will always be grateful every minute of the day for what I have. To those who think I have or that I will change, I have one thing to say… Shut up!

# AMYISMS

Don't understand some of my Essex lingo? Don't worry, gorge, because I've put together a little dictionary for you and it'll all become crystal\*. 😮

**A BIT OF ME**
Something that would interest me, e.g. 'He's a bit of me.'

**AGG**
Abbreviation of aggravates, which means to annoy and make a situation worse or more troublesome e.g. 'Too much agg.'

OR

**AGGY**
An extended abbreviation of 'agg' meaning an annoying situation or someone that aggravates.

**AMAZE**
Abbreviation of 'amazing' meaning to cause great surprise or wonder; astonishing.

## BANG OUT OF ORDER

To be completely wrong, unfair, un-called-for or ridiculous, e.g. 'He's bang out of order for cheating on her.'

## BEHAVE – pronounced 'be'ave'

To behave yourself and not be silly: usually a reaction to a stupid comment or something you cannot believe e.g. 'Oh behave!'

## BTW

An abbreviation for 'by the way'.

## CLOCK

A slang word for explaining that you've spotted someone, e.g. 'I have just clocked that famous man in the salon.'

## CRINGE

Cringe is the word to describe the feeling of extreme embarrassment felt at an awkward or uncomfortable situation – derives from a specific genre of comedy, *Cringe* comedy where the intent is to make you uncomfortable rather than make you laugh.

## CRYSTAL

An abbreviation of the phrase 'crystal clear'.

## DO ONE

To 'do one' is to leave the vicinity: a term usually used in an argument, e.g. 'Why don't you just do one?!'

## GET OFF WITH
To kiss or French-kiss someone.

## GORGE
Abbreviation of 'gorgeous'; to be beautiful and very attractive, e.g. 'She's a gorge girl.'

## GORGIES
Abbreviation of 'gorgeous' meaning to be beautiful and very attractive.

## GRILL
A modern word used to describe a face or mouth.

## THE HUMP (pronounced 'thc 'ump')
A phrase used to express getting upset/annoyed with someone because you think they have done something bad to you.

## JIP
To give someone trouble, e.g. 'she's giving me jip.'

## KICK OFF
When a fight or argument starts, e.g. 'It's all going to kick off over there.'

## LAIRY
British slang for displaying an aggressive attitude in order to provoke a fight, argument or any verbal or physical

confrontation. Lairing someone up is like winding them up, maliciously.

## LOL
An abbreviation of 'laugh out loud' or 'laughing out loud.' Used mainly in electronic communication to draw attention to a joke or to express amusement. Occasionally used for 'Lots Of Love.'

## MAJOR
Meaning a really big deal and most commonly used within a sentence, for example – 'It was always a major event' or 'it was major'.

## MINGING
An adjective that means very bad or unpleasant.

## MOTOR
Slang for car or any other kind of motorised vehicle.

## MUGGED OFF
To be mugged off means that you are being made a fool of by someone taking advantage of you. To mug someone is to take something by force.

## MUGGY
From the root 'mug', meaning to be a fool (which originally derived from the standard English 'mug', i.e. that into which

one can pour something, as in this case it is filled with false information).

## NIP SHOTS
A photograph of nipples.

## NOON
Slang word for female genitalia.

## NORM
An abbreviation of the word 'normal'.

## OBVS
Abbreviation of 'obviously' meaning in a way that is easily perceived or understood; clearly.

## ON IT
To get on it or 'have it' is an expression generally used when you have to fit a certain criteria in a social group. Examples include getting intoxicated when going out with friends or dressing correctly to a work function.

## PAPPED
To be photographed by the paparazzi. Derives from the original Italian singular term 'paparazzo'. Paparazzi are freelance photographers who pursue celebrities to obtain photographs of them usually going about their daily lives.

## PAPS

An abbreviation for the paparazzi. Paparazzi are freelance photographers who pursue celebrities to obtain photographs of them usually going about their daily lives. Derived from the original Italian singular term 'paparazzo'.

## PROPER – pronounced 'propa'

Similar to 'very', 'proper' is used for emphasis, e.g. 'Proper naughty geezer.'

## REEM

The highest compliment: great, fit, attractive or perfect. Usually used to describe personal appearance, but can be used in any situation, e.g. 'That girl is well reem.' (Actually popularised by Joey Essex on *TOWIE*.)

## SERIOUS

Shortened version of 'are you serious?' – a question asked in disbelief with an extremely sarcastic tone questioning someone's actions or statement.

## SORT

An extremely attractive person. Originated from Cockney Rhyming Slang for a really good-looking woman.

## TBH

Abbreviation for 'to be honest'.

**TOTESVILLE**

A made-up word meaning totally.

**VAJAZZLE**

Vajazzle is a form of genital decoration, formed by the application of crystal ornaments on the shaved pubic area of a woman. The process is known as vajazzling.

**WEAPON**

To be really good-looking, e.g. 'She's a weapon!'

**WELL JEL**

Slang abbreviation of 'very jealous'. Used to express jealousy about something or of someone.